FOREWORD BY BILL C...

THINK BEYOND THE FIRST SALE

IDEA-RICH STRATEGIES TO ATTRACT REPEAT BUYERS

BOB 'IDEA MAN' HOOEY
AUTHOR, LEGACY OF LEADERSHIP

Foreword by Bill Comrie, founder The Brick

"If we all did the things we are capable of doing, we would literally astound ourselves." Thomas Edison

Someone once said, "Nothing happens until a sale is made!"

New ideas, business propositions, careers, relationships, crusades, and noble causes all happen when someone sells them. They grow and find stability when someone moves on them and thinks beyond the FIRST sale.

To all the salespeople in the world, past and present... our thanks for making our lives so much richer and rewarding.

Updated 2022

Box 10, Egremont, Alberta, Canada T0A0Z0
www.SuccessPublications.ca

Foreword by Bill Comrie

Every successful enterprise, like **The Brick**, started with a vision, an idea if you will. An idea fueled by passion and dedication that became a reality when foundations for success were built. As **The Brick** grew into Canada's largest furniture retailer and became more visible and successful, people asked me, *"How did you do it?"* or, *"What made The Brick so successful?"*

Although no longer involved, I'm still extremely proud of our 6000 Brick and United team members. I've said many times, it was these committed team members who made us so successful and profitable.

Our secret - we built solid foundations for our long-term success: an effective visionary team that provided leadership with solid organizational skills; a well-trained, enthusiastic focused sales team; **a demonstrated commitment to our customers;** active participation in the community; effective use of technology; great products of course; and supportive employee relationships. We built an aggressive marketing team with innovative ideas. We were the first to have a Midnight Madness sale. We were the first company in the world to offer a no interest payment plan with same day delivery. Now you can see why we confidently declared **"Nobody beats The Brick!"**

I met Canadian Ideaman, **Bob Hooey** while our President **Kim Yost** was interviewing writers for a project. We told Bob if he helped our teams be more productive, he could live there at The Brick. His response, *"I'm not sure I'd want to live here, but I would love to visit on a regular basis."* And for many years, he *did just that,* as we tapped into his creativity and commitment to our team for various projects.

Bob lives his *'Think beyond the first sale'* focus. From day one he demonstrated his willingness to help us better equip our leaders and teams to reach and expand our goals. He helped all of us at Team Brick become even better! Thanks, Bob! His first project was working with our President Kim Yost and 22 VPs over 4 months on areas like leadership development, succession planning, time management, inter-departmental co-operation, motivation, and even enhanced sales projections. He challenged them to **THINK *BIGGER*,** way past the initial sales goal, if we wanted to break the billion-dollar retail benchmark. They *'got it'* and we went on to shatter the billion-dollar level over the next year.

We tapped into his creative mindset to create **THE BRICK WAY** as a venue to share our culture, cross-train, and motivate between departments. Following a lunch with our President Kim Yost, Bob came up with an internet-based sales training program concept for our teams across the country. **Secret Selling Tips** successfully created ongoing training, tips, techniques, and motivation for our Canadian sales teams.

Personally, he helped me craft my speeches when I was surprised and honored as Alberta Businessman of the Year, Canadian Retailer of the Year, Canada's Entrepreneur of the year, and even an honorary doctorate. His insights helped me focus and deliver my message more effectively. He was very much a coach, friend, and encourager to me.

He has a great sales sense. He surprised me when we were working on a speech for the Alberta Home Builders Association by saying, *"Bill, you're leaving money on the table!"* I looked interested. He went on to explain, *"These are your prospective customers and a solid market for your stores."* He was right! We gathered our leadership and developed a special display home offer which effectively turned numerous display homes across Alberta into Mini-Brick promotional centers.

When you **THINK Beyond the FIRST Sale** you create a conversation with your customer that keeps them engaged and coming back again and again. Bob does! This is a profitable long-term secret of very successful companies who realize and tap into the lifetime value of their clients. It certainly was mine as I founded and built Team Brick. Put Bob's innovative Ideas at Work with your team and see your sales and business succeed.

© **Bill Comrie**, *is a Canadian businessman, founder of The Brick, one of Canada's largest volume retailers of furniture, mattresses, appliances and home electronics; former Edmonton Oil Kings captain, Edmonton Eskimos board member, B.C. Lions owner, San Diego Gulls owner, and part-owner of the 2016 World Series Champion Chicago Cubs.*

Dedicated to our clients, who may choose, at times, to be our 'customers'

Perhaps you will notice that we do not *exclusively* refer to 'customers' in this publication, choosing instead to employ the descriptive word 'clients'. This is a deliberate word choice in our vocabulary and a foundational change in mindset necessary to move beyond the FIRST sale into a long-term mutually beneficial relationship with your clients.

Client vs. Customer: Aren't they really the same thing? Webster's defines these two seemingly interchangeable words as:

Customer: one that purchases a commodity or service

Client: one that is 'under the protection' of another; a person who engages the professional advice or services of another

Ever wondered why the sales superstars sell so much better and make so much more money than their counterparts? One secret is in how they visualize and more effectively approach everyone, which results in such high levels of success. They see clients, vs. customers, walk into their locations and act accordingly.

Take a moment and reflect on the differences in the meanings of these two words. The way a person, who does business with you, can be approached and treated will directly impact your results.

In the past, you may have referred to them as customers. In fact, when I started writing Secret Selling Tips (2006), I initially called them 'customers' to align with typical retail terminology used by our first national client. We transitioned back to 'Clients' with an explanation of our sales philosophy and our THINK Beyond the First Sale programs in year two. I had for years, prior to starting Secret Selling Tips, thought of them as clients; partly from the many years of serving my design clients who came to me for help in creating the kitchen of their dreams. I learned that as well from my connections with leading selling professionals across North America. Perhaps it would be a profitable idea for you to follow their lead.

The key to this mental shift lies in understanding what **'under the protection'** of another means in your client interactions.

My thought: this means you don't sell someone a service or product 'just' to ensure you make the largest short-term profit or commission possible. You **serve them best** by helping them *fully* explore their options to make the *'best choice'* when they purchase something!

Even if they are not able to articulate what results they need, it is important that you, as the selling professional, understand and appreciate exactly what your clients need when they do business with you and your company. The better you do that, the more you will succeed over the long-term. This service or client protection mentality also builds solid repeat and referral business for you.

Once you figure out what outcome or benefit is needed (solid qualifying skills), you can gently lead them to that outcome. You become their solutions provider as well as their trusted guide. When you do, you become a high trust professional advisor who serves and protects them. This builds a foundation for them to remain your client for life and to become your biggest fan. It also builds a foundation for a long-term valuable client friendship.

"I have never worked a day in my life without selling. If I believe in something, I sell it, and I sell it hard." **Estée Lauder**

In previous sales success publications, we've shared that research shows people 'still' like to do business with those they trust and like. That research remains true in 2017. **One secret to selling success** is to maximize each client relationship by ensuring you demonstrate your commitment to helping them, not just selling them. That mental shift is reinforced when you think of them as 'valued' clients not 'just' customers.

The end-result is they will buy from you again and encourage their friends and contacts to follow their lead in selecting you to serve them.

From all of us at **Success Publications**, we wish you the very best for your quest to become and remain a top serving salesperson and for the productive years that follow.

We wish you all the success in selling you could imagine and all that you can create by applying these ideas. In the past two years, we have updated, re-written, and re-released our success publications to help those top performing leaders, sales professionals and business owners. Perhaps a few of them should be in your success library. **www.SuccessPubilcations.ca** for more information and ordering.

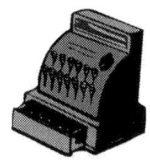

Idea-rich service as a sales tool for higher prices

If you are looking for a way to differentiate yourself from your completion and minimize having to offer discounts, exceptional customer service works. More so if you happen to be a smaller company (or project that smaller, friendly image to your prospective clients). As reported in a 2011 **American Express** survey 80% of North Americans thought that smaller companies placed a greater emphasis on customer service. In that same survey respondents indicated (70%) they were willing to spend more with companies they believed provide excellent customer service. They also mentioned (59%) they'd try a new brand or company if it provided a better customer service experience.

Think about who you do business with now. *For example, I drive out of my way to use a dry cleaner that treats me specially. There are several other vendors that get my business because of their service. I don't mind the difference in price, because I know what I am getting and I like it, and I like them.*

As reported in a Customer Experience Impact report by **Harris Interactive**, 90% indicated they would pay 'more' to ensure they got a superior customer service.

Even if you are a BIG-BOX type of operation, simply competing on price is not the most effective way to build or sustain your business. Exceptional service delivered each time is a great defense against even the toughest competition — customer service that provides what they really need, delivered with expertise and a great attitude. Make them feel special, treat them right, and they will come back to you and bring their friends.

Table of Contents

Foreword by Bill Comrie 3
Dedicated to our clients, who may choose, at times, to be our 'customers'. 5
Table of Contents 8
A word as we continue our journey together 10
Ideas to get the 'best' from 'THINK Beyond the First Sale' 13
Advancing your sales techniques 17
How to turn their 'initial' purchase into repeat business 22
Out of sight - Out of mind – Out of business! 24
Exploring solutions to 'Show and Sell'. 27
Winning at Retail – lessons to leverage 33
Creating time to sell – invest in your future success 36
Little hinges swing big doors 40
Building a successful sales career or profitable business 41
Mistakes made by NEW, lazy, or ineffective sales staff 45
Eight tips to dramatically increase your sales income 48
How to turn your sales into profitable repeat business 52
Five successful techniques for generating increased sales 56
Problems 59
An idea-rich KEY to generating repeat sales 60
What makes 'YOU-nique?'. 63
Reasons people buy and keep on buying 64
Client service redefined… as a sales success tool 67
Would you buy from yourself? 70
Asking the right questions and finding qualified clients 73
Qualifying 'continued' as a crucial step in your success 75
Finding your ideal client 78
Getting client feedback using surveys 80
Rules of Value-Added selling and Top Level service 83
Building foundations for a successful sale 86
Tell descriptive, idea-rich stories that engage our minds, create value, and help sell on more than one level 87
How to Up Sell for increased sales and commissions 90
Proactive strategies to minimize price objections 92
Checkpoints for Super Sales techniques 95
Build your ABC account management data base 97
Idea-rich secrets to getting great word of mouth referrals and repeat sales 98

Getting your customers to sell you... Creating fans and champions 99
Go the extra mile – inspired action to separate yourself from your competition 100
Delivering quality and getting repeat orders.. 102
The ABC System of effective account management......................... 105
Getting your clients to sell you... 107
Unhappy customers cost you money – lots of money!..................... 109
Principles of power negotiating techniques... 111
A 60 second reminder... 113
I'm the nice customer... who never comes back! 116
Thanks for reading 'THINK Beyond the First Sale'........................... 117
About the author 118
Copyright and license notes 121
Acknowledgements, credits, and disclaimers 122
Disclaimer.. 123
Bob's B.E.S.T. publications 124
What they say about Bob 'Idea Man' Hooey...................................... 126
Engage Bob for your leaders and their teams 128

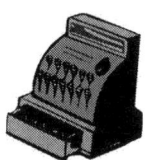

PRO-Tips: We will be seeding sales tips from top performing sales experts and trainers from around the globe throughout the book. People like my friends, Jim Cathcart, Tony Alessandra, Patricia Fripp, Ray Leone, Patti Pokorchak, Joe Bonura, Peter Chapman, Jeff Mowatt, Stu Shultz, Ken Keis, Kim Duke, Tim Breithaupt, Terry Brock, Patrick Leroux, and Sylvia Perreault.

A word as we continue our journey together

"Sales can be a tough and sometimes complex, challenging, and confusing profession. It can also be fun!"

As a top performing professional salesperson, you need to identify individuals and organizations which you think may be interested in your product or service.

You approach people who may or may not want to talk to you. When the opportunity to meet with a prospective client arises, you need to convince them that your product or service is better and/or more cost effective than your competitors! You work diligently to build relationships. You may even close the sale! **Remember: this is just the beginning of the sales journey!**

Then, you work hard to keep your clients satisfied. You strive to earn their trust and secure their consideration of you for future or repeat sales. The rewards, both financial and professional are tremendous.

As tough as the sales profession is, there are ways to improve your chances of long-term success. The overall sales process can be broken down into manageable and measurable steps.

Understanding each of these steps and following them can help you realize the maximum benefits from your sales efforts.

We are very familiar with the business of sales. Our instructors, guest authors, and facilitators have been in the sales trenches for many years. They know, firsthand, the areas of opportunity as well as the pitfalls. We have given enhanced selling workshops and keynotes to thousands of professionals, just like you, across the globe with excellent results. Our online **Secret Selling Tips** *sales success program has been successfully used in advancing sales techniques for thousands of sales professionals across North America.*

THINK Beyond the 'FIRST' Sale – Idea-rich strategies to attract repeat buyers. When applied, these strategies create repeat buyers for top performing sales professionals and builds on the first two publications of our professional Sales Success Series.

We are confident that, by the end of this *sales success workbook*, you will have had the opportunity to access a substantial amount of information to help make you a better, more confident sales professional who knows how to 'Attract Repeat Buyers'. Notice we call it a workbook because we challenge you to do the point-to-ponder exercises to move forward in your careers.

We trust you will also continue building a solid base of satisfied clients who will refer you on a regular basis. This sales success workbook was originally written for use with a program for a national seminar company and was personally delivered by the author across Canada in 2003 and 2004. *I had intended on updating it and expanding it with some of the examples and personal stories used in those workshops. Now I have, again (2022)! Enjoy!*

I trust you will enjoy our ideas and apply them to gain increased success in your efforts. Perhaps you and your team would invite me to present it in person at your location. I'd love to share with you in person. www.HaveMouthWillTravel.com

Advancing your sales techniques by honing your selling and service skills is your best method to earning more money and building solid repeat business. The future you create can be great and it can be very profitable as you apply these idea-rich sales strategies with your clients!

Bob 'Idea Man' Hooey
www.ideaman.net
www.bobhooey.training

 Visit: www.SuccessPublications.ca/BusinessSuccess-Tips.html for special business building success video tips.

11

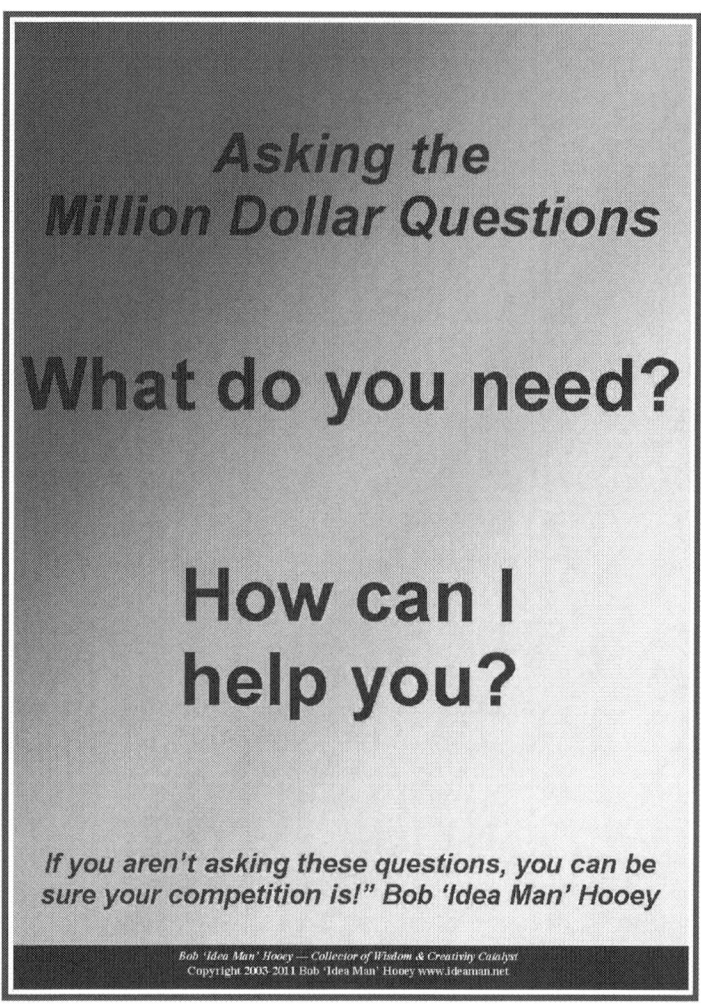

Foundational hint: Asking the right questions, the questions that open conversations with your prospective clients are a key to your long-term success as a top performing salesperson. They are also strategic in building and enhancing any business or organization. Know what they need and design something creative to better serve them. That is where the sales magic happens.

"You don't need a big close, as many sales reps believe. You risk losing your customer when you save all the good stuff for the end. Keep the customer actively involved throughout your presentation, and watch your results improve." Harvey Mackay

Ideas to get the 'best' from 'THINK Beyond the First Sale'

'THINK Beyond the First Sale' – Idea-rich strategies to attract repeat buyers contains a range of tips, techniques, and ideas to help you improve the way you 'train' and lead your team for shared growth and profitable long-term success with your clients. It evolved into its present format (from a college level program) with the inclusion of stories, ideas, and first-hand experience based on conversations, copious notes, and first-hand observations of productive fellow leaders, sales professionals, and successful retailers. It was made personal from my own experiences in leading and being on a variety of teams across North America and the globe. It is seasoned with my own sales and customer service tips and experiences in retail, direct sales, and professional services.

It has been updated (2017 and 2022) with a focus to assist professionals, owners, and leaders more profitably enhance their business with enhanced customer service. It is designed as a guide for those who want to take personal leadership over their own lives and actions; providing a purpose and making a positive contribution in the lives of their teams and interaction with their clients.

This is not just a book for casual reading. It is a book to be *chewed*, to be dipped into, and leveraged as a resource or reference guide. It is a workbook with provocative questions that help you decide what you want to accomplish with your life, your leadership, and with your client and team relationships. It is your resource, so mark it, highlight it, and make notes in the margins.

To get the best from this book, first visit the Table of Contents to identify which chapters and/or topics meet your most critical, time sensitive needs. Read them carefully and make sure you understand the guidelines and advice given. Some of the topics may not be of direct interest to you (now) depending on your needs. You may wish to read some of the other chapters so that you can understand the needs of other leaders, 'client' or customer sales/service scenarios.

'THINK Beyond the First Sale' does not contain ALL the answers. It contains a collection of thoughts, notes, clippings, tips, techniques, lessons learned, and ideas shared primarily from one learner, one business leader's (one retailer's) viewpoint, mine.

It is simply intended as an aid to your reflection, learning, and inspiration – a resource that you can draw upon. Its aim is to give you a creative resource that, when applied and practiced with your teams, will help you develop and build both your confidence and profitable competence as a sales leader, manager, and business owner.

A more productive approach would be to take the tips and concepts presented here and blend them with your own sales leadership style, personality, and creativity. Keep in mind your own time constraints and 'comfort zone' as a sales leader, manager, or professional. Generate unique and perhaps personalized ideas on how you can create, give, and improve your interaction and action with your teams.

'THINK Beyond the First Sale' – 3rd **edition** is designed to offer you flexibility in how you leverage it for your personal and professional use.

1) You can easily sit down for an hour or two and read it **cover-to-cover**. This is a great way to start by getting a feel for what is included, especially for newer or emerging leaders, managers, or owners (those who want to take more personal leadership for their lives and better equip their teams to grow) who want to gain the full benefit from their investment.

A word of advice: *'THINK Beyond the First Sale'* is the result of 29 plus years of personal study, first-hand experience, and observation in a variety of leadership, retail, business, and sales roles; as well as coaching and support and coaching roles for executive clients and their respective teams. It might seem overwhelming or confusing at first with the range of information included here. Once you have done a quick read of the whole book, identify sections or tips that interest you and work on manageable chunks.

2) You can select one chapter or section and work to incorporate the ideas you discover into your own specific leadership role, client engagement, or business situation.

3) You can look at the Table of Contents and jump straight to the tips or areas of study that particularly interest you.

We have attempted to incorporate something of benefit for everyone, regardless of your current level or skill in business. You might even find some *contradictory* advice in different parts of the book! ☺ This is because there is no single, universal 'right answer' – you must find what is a right fit for you, your objective, and your team's specific needs.

What works for you is what is best. Choose it, try it, and adapt it as needed to serve you in your quest to be a more effective businessperson and impactful leader. Take control of how you allocate, invest, or leverage your time and interaction with your staff and clients. We've written it to help you guide your teams to become more productive and profitably enhance your business dealings with your clients.

Master, who is my customer?

Many years ago, a young servant came to his master and enquired of him how he should be successful in business. The wise Master said, ***"By taking care of the real needs and providing true value for your customers."*** The young servant replied, ***"But Master, who is my customer?"***

This parable, adapted from my Sunday school days illustrates the confusion we all too often have in work or business. ***"Who is your customer?"*** I would contend that we have *'internal'* and *'external'* customers.

Both are important to your success! Without satisfied external customers you have no business, and without involved and committed internal customers you will lose it to your competition.

External customers are those who would do or continue to do business with us and allow us to make a profit.
• Why would it be important to make sure we take care of the needs of our external customers?
• What can you do to ensure they are taken care of effectively and completely?

Internal customers are those who assist us in making our business successful by playing a part or supplying something we need to be successful ...our management team, co-workers, suppliers, and sub-contractors.
• The same question on taking care of our internal customer's needs requires a bit more thought, doesn't it?
• Why would it make sense to take care of those who work alongside you in your business, or do part of the sales, delivery, service, or installation process? To your customer, **'they' are the company** and each time they encounter one of them, your reputation and referral factor is on the line.

Why would it make sense to take care of those who supply you with products or services? **None of us work in isolation**, do we?
• In a pinch when you *"just gotta have it!"* - whom do you think your suppliers will help? Perhaps the person who has *consistently* treated them well?
• Why would that be? (skill testing question here)
• What can you do to build a relationship that returns a positive response?
• What are you committed to doing to increase your effectiveness in serving your external customers and internal customers alike?
• When will you implement it? Act soon to protect your career investment!

Smart businesses and career-focused employees learn to focus their energies on making sure the internal and external customers are taken care of and satisfied. **This is the secret of building a super successful business or productive career!**

Alfredo is 'my' plumber, my go to guy for at least 10 years when I need something fixed or installed (2 bathrooms, kitchen, hot water heater, etc.) who is prompt, friendly, and really knows his stuff. He is also a friendly guy and I wouldn't think of hiring someone else. His wife, **Ursula** had the ***Crimson Creek Café*** in nearby Redwater. She made everyone feel welcome and takes time to 'sell' the new additions to their coffee and sandwich collections. This was become my place to drop in for a break in my routine, until she closed down a couple of years back due to her health. Both knew – service sells!

Advancing your sales techniques
Idea-rich strategies to attract repeat buyers

Being and remaining successful in the sales game means making the best use of your time and increasing the overall volume of profitable sales you bring into your company. Successful, top-level sales professionals know this and 'deliberately' focus their energies on the most important aspects of the selling process – acquiring, serving, and keeping their clients.

Please note: We refer to **Top Performing Sales Professionals** throughout this publication because that is who we have studied, and that is our desire for you.

For most businesses, the costs associated with acquiring a new client are about 5 to 10 times greater than securing an order from an existing client. Yet most companies and many ineffective salespeople neglect the more profitable, long-term relationships with their current clientele; choosing instead to focus their energy on prospecting – attempting to close new clients.

- **New clients provide growth.**
- **Mining existing clients provides profit and sustained, long-term growth.**

In this sales success workbook (*we chose workbook for a reason – it is meant for you to work though, not just read*) we will investigate 'why' and 'how' you should act if creating repeat buyers is your sales success goal. We will outline tools and techniques which have been field-proven by North America's top performing sales professionals. Tools you can apply – and profit from – tomorrow when you return to your sales environment.

In business, there are three main approaches to increasing your business and gaining increased sales results:

- **Increase the number** of clients;
- **Increase the average size of the sale** per client;
- **Increase the frequency** at which a client returns to buy again.

There are many great sales books on the market. My friend **Brian Tracy** has written many of them, including *'The Art of Closing the Sale.'* This sales success workbook will focus primarily on tools and techniques which target the second two approaches. It will help you more effectively pre-qualify your prospects by evaluating their lifetime value as a client. Marketing (focusing on increasing the number of clients) is also important and we'll share a few ideas on that as we work through this publication.

Not surprisingly, focusing on the second two approaches, with an emphasis on ensuring that your current clients receive exceptional client satisfaction, will subsequently generate new clients. People love to share a good experience and will start selling or referring you to their friends and business associates. Success tends to expand and spread!

This is the best used secret we've observed in top performers and their organizations. It will help you to develop a simple account management system focused on increased sales and overall account growth. Once this account management system is in place, you will be able to direct your energies on the clients who will profitably grow with you; and, by so doing, realize your maximum potential as a committed selling professional.

As reported by a Boston based consulting firm, the average Fortune 500 Company could instantly double its revenue growth rate with a 5% increase in client retention, and a small to mid-size company could double its profits in ten years by simply increasing its client retention rate by 5%. Research results draw an interesting parallel in process, timeline, and results for profitability in small, mid-size, and larger firms. People buy for various reasons and buying often has an emotional attachment.

Knowing and understanding the emotions behind the various reasons why people buy will allow you to position or re-position yourself and your company to provide additional products and services over an extended period. Applied knowledge delivers real selling power.

A few thoughts on setting sales success goals, 'even' in tough times Ultimately, the *measurement and review of your value* to your firm, as a salesperson, is directly tied to your ability to sell.

Your leadership team will look at your sales volume at a specific time during your firm's term of measurement. That look might be monthly, quarterly, a bi-yearly performance appraisal, or year end. But it will happen, and it makes good sense to be both aware of it and prepare to ensure your sales results *stand up* under scrutiny.

You may be providing intrinsic value to your team and your firm by your activities. However, when all is said and done, your sales results are the primary factor used to evaluate your performance and promotion. That is the harsh truth.

Sales master **W. Clement Stone** challenged his sales team to ***"Set a goal so BIG, that if you achieved it, it would blow your mind."***

This is not a time to play it safe, nor is it time to listen to those (even those who may be relatively successful in selling) who would tell you setting goals is a waste of time. It isn't a waste of your time. Your success and growth in the sales field will be directly tied to your ability to formally set and achieve your goals.

Set a realistic goal that will push you; one that will stretch you in its achievement. Set a goal worthy of your potential and then work diligently to achieve it. **Prepare yourself to win!**

In sales, life, and business we have proven results and thousands of stories of people who formally set goals who went on to substantially greater success than their counterparts. You can too, if you *'plan and then work your plan.'* This investment of your time in setting your goals for the year, and revisiting and revising them as needed, provides the roadmap for your sales success; *'more so'* in tough times when every sale counts.

Take a few minutes and go through a brief planning process considering your **BIG Goal**. Depending on your focus (sales, commission, units) here is how you might do it.

1. Set your income or sales target (choose which works best for you) or,
2. Set your commission and/or bonus target (if this works better for you) or,

3. Divide your yearly target (#1) by the average commission and/or bonus per sale (#2). If you need help, go back over your previous year or talk to your sales manager. This calculation should yield an annual 'unit' sales target needed to reach your sales target, income, or commission.
4. You can then divide this number (either #1, #2, #3) by 12 to give your monthly target, or divide it by 50 (average number of weeks with 2 weeks of holidays) to get your weekly number.

See it! Write it! Achieve it!

However, you work it out, it is a good idea to break your 'BIG' sales goal into measurable weekly and/or monthly results. That makes it easier to track your success and make changes if you notice you need to bump it up to keep on track. My friend, **Marc LeBlanc** suggests making every month a symbolic New Year.

Now what?

What is next if you are serious about meeting this BIG goal?

- What activities (average) do you need to be involved in on a weekly or monthly basis to reach your calculated results?
- How many outbound sales calls do you need to make to explore or set up an initial sales interview?
- How many (average) sales interviews or demonstrations (daily, weekly, monthly, quarterly) do you need to qualify a customer where an order can be placed, or a proposal created?
- How many (average) proposals or contracts need to be delivered daily (weekly, monthly, and quarterly) to close the deal?

If needed, you can go back over your last year's results (keep in mind you are setting a big goal that will stretch you) to get a sense of what is needed to get to the sale. When you have worked out your sales numbers in relation to your BIG sales goal, then you are ready. Being prepared is one of the Secrets to being successful in sales.

Henry Ford said, *"Before everything else, being ready is the Secret of Success!"*

Keep these numbers close to you as a reference guide to chart your progress. Measure them frequently and honestly and decide where you need help. Ask for help when you need it.

- Do you need help in prospecting or qualifying?
- Do you need help demonstrating your firm's products or explaining your firm's services, policies, etc.?
- Do you need help in closing?
- Do you need help in follow up to create additional sales and repeat business?

As you go through this process it may become apparent that you need to invest in your own development as a selling professional. That is good! Over the centuries, our top sales leaders were people who realized the importance of investing in their future success, today! Their preparation allowed them to productively weather economic upheavals, storms, and tough times.

Johann Friedrich von Schiller wrote, *"The average estimate themselves by what they do, the above average by what they are."*

PRO-tips: When business is slow shake the tree.
What tree? All of your past customers are the tree. If you have done a good job for them, then they trust you. Developing trust is the most difficult challenge we have with new prospects. You already have it with past clients. In addition, you have credibility. I recently received an email from the president of a trade association. He said that he had attended a program I did 25 years ago, in Puerto Rico and his sales had gone from $2 million to $21 million! Now that he is president of the association, he recommended me for their annual convention. (I got the gig). But I should have contacted him, not the other way around. How much business is out there that we are leaving on the table?

Send an email to all past clients and say, *"I need your help. Who do you know that could benefit from my services?"* or offer them a new product or service. © **Ray Leone** www.wholebrainselling.com

How to turn their 'initial' purchase into repeat business

Most sales driven organizations are so preoccupied getting 'new' customers; they pay little attention to their existing customers. It is an expensive mistake when you let them 'slip away' as you have essentially just wasted your money and your efforts in getting them in the first place.

You see, by investing time on generating repeat business from your existing (clients) customers you and your company will reap the following benefits:

- You save on advertising costs to get a new customer in the first place.
- They need your product/service, so they are your continuing target market.
- You can have a more effective mail out for follow up contacts and add on sales.
- You can ask them what they want and then you seek to satisfy them.
- If they are happy with you and your organization, they will tell others – leverage the power of word-of-mouth.
- You can make your existing customers an offer which can include their friends, family, and colleagues.

Because your firm has already spent a substantial portion of your advertising money on attracting a new customer; it makes good sense (and dollars too) to work at keeping that customer once they have made a purchase.

"I think there is something more important than believing: Action! The world is full of dreamers, there aren't enough who will move ahead and begin to take concrete steps to actualize their vision." W. Clement Stone

For your sales career to grow and be successful, you need to ACT to develop a growing relationship with your existing customers, so they understand that your business is looking after them.

If they have already bought from you then they are your target market – so don't forget them. The chances are (70% according to a Harris Interactive survey), if they are happy with your business, they will buy from you again. They just need reminding of the benefits that your business can offer them.

Remember, out-of-sight leads to out-of-mind which can lead to out-of-business.

What does it cost you to acquire a 'new' customer? Ask your Chief Financial Officer (CFO) for this figure: $_____ Often that figure is 6-10 times the cost of keeping a current customer and expanding the business they do with you.

Challenge: To help you measure your potential to secure repeat business, ask yourself these questions:
- How good is your personal and your company's customer service?
- Have you got systems in place to ensure consistency of service and product development?
- Are you happy with your image – are you relaying the 'right' message?
- What does your organisation do for customers that your competitors are not doing?
- Do you make the most of the testimonials from your satisfied customers to keep the momentum going?
- Have your promotional activities in place which targets your existing customers, and which makes them 'feel' valued and special?
- Do you survey your existing customers to help expand or improve your Product or service to them?

So, how did you rate? Believe it or not there's much more to know when it comes to maximizing your sales potential for repeat business. Keep your existing customers coming back for more and getting them to 'spread the word' about your business.

Out of sight - Out of mind – Out of business!

Building a long-term profitable sales career and/or business is built on acquiring and taking care of your clients. Many clients simply get ignored, forget who they bought their product or service from, or simply drift away. This can be devastating to your profit margins.

To avoid this happening to you, please do this:
- Create a simple, yet systematic, process that will keep you in the top-of-mind position as a value-added resource to your clients.
- Remind them of their importance to you and your firm and learn ways to creatively touch base and market to them again and again.

What are you doing to help your valued clients remember you?

When I worked in the kitchen design field, I created little brass plaques that were installed, at eye level, on one of the more focal cabinets in the kitchen. Each 1" x 3" plaque had my client's name as well as mine and my company's. This generated interest, expressed professionalism, and helped with amazing referrals. If I was doing that today, it would have my website listed as well.

In our speaking and training business (Ideas At Work! www.ideaman.net or www.BobHooey.training) we offer follow up e-zines, special offers, Thanksgiving cards, as well as Christmas cards, and a number of other means to keep in touch. We want to ensure that our clients don't forget us. We ensure that any piece of paper we share has our contact information included, so they can find us later.

Client service is a critical foundation for continued relationship and increased long-term sales potential. Keep your clients satisfied and they will continue to purchase from you. It is a simple concept, but often missed by average companies and sales staff.

In a recent study which polled 6000 clients:
- 95% were willing to be repeat clients because of the excellent service and products they received;
- after receiving good service (acceptable but not impressive), the numbers dropped to 62%;
- upon receiving only fair service and products, 7% were willing to return with their business; and

- none of the clients who received poor goods or services would consider doing business with that vendor again.

You do the math!

Remember, satisfied clients become fans and champions for you and your firm and can dynamically increase your overall sales. The impact of treating our best clients well is staggering. Over the years, I have been very fortunate to have earned the trust and referrals from many of my clients. These referrals have allowed me to expand my business globally and to extend my service to a whole range of new clients and industries.

In a Harvard Business Review article, **Alan Grant** and **Leonard Schlesinger** wrote: *"Given the fixed cost structure of a grocery store, the contribution margin from each client dollar spent can earn 10 times the store's net profit margin. Thus, the company found that even small improvements in any one of the client behaviours led to very significant profitability gains.*

Expanding the client base by two percent with primary shoppers, for example, would increase the store's profitability by more than 45%. Converting just 200 secondary clients into primary shoppers would increase the profitability by 20 per cent. Persuading every client to substitute two store-brand items for two national-brand items each time they visited the store would increase profitability by 55 percent."

There is a value-added lesson for each of us as top performing sales professionals in taking care of our primary clients and mining our secondary clients for repeat business. In both cases the increase in profits underscores – and pays handsomely for – the effort of doing so.

As reported by **American Demographics**, of 22 daily tasks, grocery shopping is very nearly the least popular activity we engage in. A visit to the dentist was the only activity that scored lower. Not including the time spend in transit; people spend the equivalent of two-and-a-half (work) weeks shopping each year.

A study by the US based National Retail Federation uncovered nearly half of those surveyed feel shopping is a hassle to be avoided.

A staggering 74% of men and 58% of women reported they would sometimes walk out of a store (in some cases leaving their full carts in the aisle) because they felt the wait was too long.

"Obstacles are necessary for success because in selling, as in all careers of importance, victory comes only after many struggles and countless defeats." **Og Mandino**

Does it really make sense then that the clients with the smallest number of purchases in their baskets get the express lines?

Perhaps this is what led to the creation of on-line shopping and personal shopping services as increasingly viable and profitable alternatives.

- What are the frustrations facing your clients in dealing with you (or your competitors) and what specific remedies are you working to implement to offset them?
- How are you making dealing with you a more pleasant, hassle-free experience for your clients?
- How can you make you and your company easier to do business with for your clients?

People have choices!
With the explosion of Internet based business alternatives, people have more choices globally than ever before. This creates both challenges and opportunities for those of us who are sales professionals.

- What are you doing to ensure your availability and accessibility to your clients?
- How accessible are you?
- How have you harnessed the Internet to help you serve your clients better?
- Do you offer clients Internet based service or information alongside your personal or on-site attention?
- What can you change to enhance their shopping experience?

Exploring solutions to 'Show and Sell'

"Advice is like snow; the softer it falls, the longer it dwells upon, and the deeper it sinks into the mind." Samuel Taylor Coleridge

Ander and Stern who wrote **'Winning At Retail'** defined service from a customer's perspective: (1) knowing what I want and having it in stock; (2) helping me find the product I'm looking for easily without wasting my time; (3) providing information to answer my questions and assist me in making an intelligent choice with signs, brochures, a salesperson, via the internet; and, after you've done the first three right, (4) friendly, knowledgeable staff.

Sales/Service 101: Exploring or presenting solutions

The secret to increasing your conversion and closing ratios is simple: See the process through the eyes of your client/customer. Help them make the right 'buying' decision.

This step will challenge you to do your Point-to-ponder. You need to become and remain a perceived *'knowledgeable'* expert on your product and services to fully advise and assist your customer in making the right 'buying' decision. Remember, your customer may have done their Point-to-ponder on the web before they came in to see you. They will know when you are bluffing and your credibility as well as your sales will suffer. In fact, knowing your products and services will help you ask more intelligent, differentiating questions in the qualifying stage of the selling process.

"Purpose is the engine, the power that drives and directs our lives." John Noe

We wanted to give you a *quick* overview of this critical step in the customer service/selling process. Professionals make a sale when they show or demonstrate the value and personalize or translate those features to their customers. The top performers and leading business owners are often the most knowledgeable as well.

If you have qualified well, you will already know which features to focus on and can move ahead to demonstrate their benefits and advantages to your customer.

Key to Remember: It is not the features that sell your product or service – it is those *'perceived'* benefits or advantages those features 'bring' to your customers. Thinking about and sharing from the benefit/advantage point of your customer is the secret to your long-term success in business. It is also the secret to gaining referrals and repeat business.

Simple selling formula: create a series of **'so that'** statements to help your customer.

This [**Product/Service**] has [**feature**] which means [**benefit**] 'so that' you [**advantage**].

Once you've gone through the qualifying process with your potential customer you can confidently move into the **Show and Sell** (exploring solutions) stage in helping them select the right product or service for their specific needs.

A few retail suggestions to help you successfully navigate this stage.

- **Don't overwhelm them with choices or options.** For example: if they are shopping for a TV, don't show them a TV Wall.
- Take them directly to the appropriate department or display area or discuss specific products or services of value to them.
- **One secret gleaned from top selling professionals** is to give them a choice of 3 and show them the higher/best quality or higher priced selection first. Why, you ask? People like to be in control of their choices and not overwhelmed. Giving them a choice of 3 narrows it down and allows them to 'choose' or buy. Another factor, people will often surprise you and buy the higher quality or priced choices.
- **Demonstrate hands on selling: This entails involving them and the rest of their 'buying' party** (who can have a direct influence on the decision). Get them to play with the buttons, open the drawers, change the channels in the home theatre room, lie down on a mattress, or sit on the sofa or recliner. Get them involved, let them touch it and enjoy it. Let them experience, if only for a moment, how it would feel to own and use that specific product. A great way to differentiate the features between your three choices which in the final decision.

- **Hint:** Be ready to express and demonstrate those features, benefits, and advantages that most meet their expressed and unexpressed needs. Be careful sharing your opinion. Your role as their own 'knowledgeable' advisor is that of a resource guide helping them make the right 'buying' decision for them.

This is a great opportunity to plant the seeds for an expanded sale and ongoing relationship. As you learn more about your customer you can 'logically' introduce additional components for their benefit into the mix. For example: accessories, additional pieces (e.g. TV stand), special packages or pricing (e.g. sofa, loveseat or chair; fabric protection), payment plans, protection, or warranty programs which will complement their main purchase.

Challenge: How well do you know the features, benefits, and advantages of your products and services?

- Invest time to break down and determine the more customer important features for your products and services.
- Make sure you know what benefits (to customer) each of those provide.
- Follow through to determine the advantage (to customer) for each benefit.

This is where you can access your training as well as ask your senior professionals for a little help. Preparing to meet the needs of your customers is an important part of the secret to success in selling.

Sales/Service 101: Reinforce good decisions and future service

Another secret of leading professionals is based on considering the total lifetime value of your customer. Clients/customers can, if serviced well, become long time customers, and create repeat business as well as become a great source for referrals. That crucial part of the business success process begins here, at the close of the initial purchase.

What must happen before the customer gets to enjoy the purchase, they made from you?

- Does it need to be ordered, built, delivered, set up, or serviced?
- What is involved in that process that your customer needs to know now?

Taking a minute or two to go over their purchase and what needs to happen is a good investment of their time… it is imperative from your perspective. Doing this reduces the chance they will get home and go through what we call, 'buyer's remorse'. We all go through it at times.

Your role as their *'knowledgeable'* advisor is to guide them in this process and to support their decision. That can be as simple as your honest observation, *"John, Pat… You've made a wise investment in this setting or this TV. I'm sure you'll enjoy it for years to come. Thank you for shopping here, we appreciate your business."* Or, if non-retail business, *"Thanks for your order; I'm sure it will serve you well."*

A simple thank you can work wonders in reinforcing your relationship and the good decision they made to deal with you. This is very much a personal decision, and you are part of the consideration too.

Your last 60 seconds with your client can be the most important investment in your long term, mutually profitable relationship. Invest them well. **Remember: Customers for life is a worthy goal for the sales professional.**

A few idea-rich customer service/sales tips:

- When you **say thank you**… look your customers in the eyes and 'smile'. People are so seldom *honestly thanked* it will help drive home that you are grateful for their trust and business. You should be! After all, their purchase pays your bills and allows you to take care of your family and enjoy your life, doesn't it?

- **Offer your ongoing assistance.** Make sure they don't leave without at least two of your business cards. Or, if you are calling on them make sure to leave them a couple to share. Remind them you'd appreciate them passing along your name to any of their friends or family who might also be in the market for ____. Word of mouth is a powerful marketing tool… if you prime them to use it.
- **Remind them of your firm's commitment to them and your guarantees.** Ask them to call 'you' if they have any questions. Don't use the word, 'problems' or say, *"If something goes wrong"*, as that could prime the pump for returns. Be proud, positive, and supportive of what you sell.
- If you have worked up a package or bundle for them and they did not buy the whole deal, **remind them you will keep their information on file** for future use. Let them know you'll let them know about special sales and events coming up. This primes the pump for a follow up call from you or an invitation to come in again. It also allows them to re-consider and add-on later.
- **Make sure you keep in touch.** Perhaps a quick call to see how they like their new "____", after it is delivered or set up or tried their new service, etc. This is a key success factor.
- **Walk them to the door and offer your hand.** This is a great time to personally say thanks again for shopping.
- **Help them to their car if they take purchase with them.** Go the extra mile.
- Invite them to drop back in and tell you how their purchase is working out. Tell them, *"I'd love to hear from you"*. Use your electronic customer file to keep in touch and keep them informed of events and sales that would benefit them.
- **Give them a small gift or perhaps a coupon** for a coffee and/or Danish on you at a local coffee shop. Perhaps, you can arrange with one close to your store to do so.
- Since you have their name and address, why not **take 'one' minute to pen a handwritten thank you note** (not a form or routine) and drop it in the mail on your way home. Drop another business card inside it too.

Challenge: How can you reinforce good decisions and set the foundation for future service? This might be a good topic of conversation with your fellow team members.

- Perhaps, when you are having a coffee or on that 'rare' occasion when you are standing talking to each other. Or, if you meet with colleagues (even from other businesses) from time to time.

- Come up with specific ways you can demonstrate or reinforce that your customer made a good decision.

- Come up with specific ways to generate future service and additional business or referrals.

PRO-tips: But sir, it's my duty to show you!
A few years back, I visited an authentic Indian gift shop (5 full floors) while speaking in Mumbai. After touring we were brought into a seating area and given tea. A very nice man started bringing out trays of jewellery: diamonds, emeralds, etc. He asked if I liked them and then proceeded to bring out more trays. Wow!

I made the attempt to let him know I wasn't going to buy any. His response was to shrug, smile, and say, **"But sir, it is my duty to show you!"** Twice!

Then, I made the mistake of asking if he had any garnets. Why not look, I thought? ☺

PS: My wife loved the box cut earrings and matching garnet necklace I gave her for her birthday the next week when we met in Paris on my way home. Service works as a sales tool!

© **Bob 'Idea Man' Hooey** Excerpt from "Make ME Feel Special!"

Winning at Retail – lessons to leverage

You may not be in retail sales, but we can all learn to leverage our sales efforts by exploring and learning from successful retailers. Retail is one of the most complex, challenging, and competitive business arenas in the world. The advent of a rapidly expanding global economy and the internet has made it even more so. It's no longer just a process of create interest and sell them. It's no longer just a process of advertise it and they will come. As mentioned earlier, today, being good is simply not good enough — you need to be amazing! **You need to be recognized as the best!**

One aspect that will bring you to the top, to being the best, is ensuring customer service is fully embedded in your selling process. After all:

"If you aren't taking care of your customers, your competition will!" Bob 'Idea Man' Hooey *(This quote has grown legs being included in lists, articles, etc in Fast Company, INC, and other magazines and websites across the internet.)*

If you are not constantly looking at new, innovative ways to take care of your customers, to make their experience better, to make it easier for them to do business with your company — rest assured your competition will be.

Across the globe business is changing rapidly to accommodate and assist the changing needs, desires and demands of our customers. **Susan Marthaller** counsels us to, *"Always think of your customers as suppliers first. Work closely with them, so they can supply you with the information you need to supply them with the right products and services."* Our ability to help our customers is directly related to our willingness to put ourselves in their shoes and truly see things from their perspective.

In their book, *'Winning At Retail'*, **Willard N. Ander** and **Neil Z. Stern** explore what separates the winners from the losers in retail. Their guidance is based on a long history of studying and documenting retail's biggest players and their best practices; what has worked and how can you apply it in your selling situation.

Retail's top leaders share a common drive. They've carved out a specific place in the mind of consumers by establishing or defining (at all costs) being *'the best'* at something.

Sales, with a true customer service focus, anticipates our client's needs and then re-positions ourselves to meet and exceed them.

When you decide to be *'the best'*, your staffing issues, processes, and training concerns will be challenged.

- How will your firm best equip you to effectively deal with the changes you'll experience as you re-invent yourselves?
- How can your leadership provide the necessary tools to equip you to grow and win in this challenge?

J. Marriot, Jr, of the famous Marriot hotel chain, shares, *"Motivate them, train them, care about them and make winners out of them… we know that if we treat our employees correctly, they'll treat the customers right. And if the customers are treated right, they'll come back."* We win when you win!

The 'Est' model for retail success, as introduced in *'Winning At Retail'*, encourages retail leaders to define their companies in one of five critical areas:

- **assortment** (biggest),
- **price** (cheapest),
- **fashion** (hottest),
- **customer service** (easiest),
- **speed** (quickest).

Ander and Stern defined **'service' from a customer's perspective**:

"(1) knowing what I want and having it in stock;
(2) helping me find the product I'm looking for easily without wasting my time;
(3) Providing information to answer my questions and assist me in making an intelligent choice—with signs, brochures, a salesperson, via the internet; and, after you've done the first three right,
(4) having friendly, knowledgeable people."

I would challenge you and your sales team to consider where your company can stake the claim to being the best. What will it take?

- Perhaps it will take time to make this a reality?
- Perhaps changes in your policies, procedures, and training?
- Perhaps new ideas in how you promote?
- Perhaps new ideas in how you interact with your potential customers?
- Perhaps changes in how you create and deal with the selling process itself?

"Believe in yourself! Have faith in your abilities! Without a humble but reasonable confidence in your own powers you cannot be successful or happy." Norman Vincent Peale, author of 'The Power of Positive Thinking'

With this focus in mind, you can revise your approach to selling and to serving your customers. With this focus in mind, I believe you can start Winning at Retail and in sales. I believe this will help you in your selling skills and create some amazing results in your sales figures over the next year.

PRO-tips: …it's my duty to show you! Part two
For several years, I was a rep for several eastern Canadian fabrics manufactures and importers travelling Alberta and parts of BC. Twice yearly, I would make appointments to show the new lines to fabric store owners and suggest purchases for their clientele. One thing I learned was to *not* overload or oversell them. I saw where other reps had short sightedly done this in one season only to come the next and see much of their wares still unsold on the shelves. Needless to say, they didn't make big sales in subsequent seasons.

I *strategically* worked to 'serve them best' by only selling them items we were certain would sell and make sure they were not left with old stock. This allowed us to more than double our sales moving well into the million dollar levels in subsequent years.

© Bob 'Idea Man' Hooey, www.ideaman.net

Creating time to sell – invest in your future success

The *'Creating Time to Sell, Lead, or Manage'* program was originally created and delivered for the Management Team of the **St. John Ambulance**, with all their branch managers coming together. The objective for our session was a skillful blending of solid sales, business building, and service principles with a good use of time to allow their respective teams to be more productive in their customer service efforts. It was very well received. We've spent time over the past dozen years refocusing and expanding it as a tool to offer our clients to help them succeed in attracting, profitably selling, retaining customers, and building referral and repeat business.

The secrets and tools we cover in our on-site sales, service, and management workshops have allowed top performing professionals, their managers, and their staff to find ways to be more PRO-active in successfully 'reaching' and 'retaining' clients for their organizations.

While flying to a speaking engagement in the US, I read a study that indicated the average salesperson put in a 53-hour week and this might be a low estimate. Yet, despite this long week, less than 8 hours of face-to-face sales activity was recorded (about 15%). More recently, I read that the average business owner, leader, or executive had 40-60 hours of unfinished business on their agenda at any one time. Sound familiar?

Something is radically wrong with this picture. *Work more and produce less* is not a good indicator for any organization that wants to survive or thrive in an extremely hectic and competitive market. Whatever happened to *'work smarter not harder'*? We are too busy, overwhelmed, and distracted, and that impacts our ability to serve and sell to our clients.

We are too busy to invest the necessary time training our staff in their effort to be equipped to succeed. **We are too busy to truly enhance our business and generate all the sales potentially available.** Sad, really!

Creating more face-to-face time for the sales and marketing process will give you an amazing (ROI) return on your investment. Focus on how you can free up your time to invest in activities that will advance your sales results and build long-term mutually beneficial client relationships. If you want to be more successful in the game of selling, you need to free up time so you can actually be 'IN' the game of selling.

We'll give you tips to help you acquire some simple priority (time) management skills which can easily help free up to 2 hours per day to contact and serve your existing clients; and of course, capture some new profitable ones along the way.

Before we dive in further, let's take a moment and brainstorm some ideas or reasons why you would like to discover new ways to create repeat buyers for your firm. Explore 'why' you would like to create add-on orders and/or have clients thank you for up-selling them.

Ask yourself; no, decide to track and analyze exactly how much time you 'actually' spend in the sales/customer service process. The results will surprise you and they may even scare you! Many of us in the sales /customer service field find ourselves easily sidetracked. We spend time doing 'paperwork', filling out reports or 'busy work', chatting on the phone, chatting with our colleagues, reading the paper, taking long breaks, and other such 'non-productive' activities.

Am I saying to eliminate these in their entirety? NO! Simply be aware of where you invest your time – and track the results to ensure that investment is well placed. You **'make money'** in business primarily when you are in face-to-face or phone-to-phone sales or follow up contact with your clients. You **'earn that money'** by delivering on what you contract and you **'leverage that money'** by good client contact and ongoing service. But first, you need to be and/or keep in contact with them.

- **Prospecting** is good use of time in the sales/customer service process – how much time do you spend doing it? Have you developed a systematic way to track and follow up on each one?
- Do you set-aside specific times (each day / week /month) to contact potential or former clients? When?
- Have you set aside specific times to maintain contact with existing clients to find out when and where you can help them again? **Repeat sales are the best** and the most profitable ones! *I love it when a client I've spoken for calls and asks me to come again. Referrals don't hurt the process either! Many of my clients hear about me from another client, speaker, or trainer and then call to see if I can help their teams.*
- Have you set aside specific time for follow up, to make sure your current clients received what you promised and are satisfied with their relationship with you?

According to **Marketing Metrics** your probability of selling to existing customers is 60-70% whereas your probability with new prospects is only 5-20%. The **White House Office of Consumer Affairs** states that loyal customers are worth up to 10 times as much as their initial purchase. Factor in acquiring new clients is 6-7 times more expensive than keeping existing ones and you'll start seeing the value of maintaining good customer service.

Disciplined customer service is a crucial SALES success tool for the top performing professional, business owner, and champion salesperson. It amazes them when you call – so few salespeople do! It helps convert them into your champions and fans when you follow-up and ensure they are happy. When you find out early when something is not working correctly or needs adjustment, fix it!

- Have you worked to make it easier for your clients to find you, get the information they need, and track their order or service process? UPS and FEDEX use on-line tracking systems, which is really a very effective sales and marketing tool. **Michael Hammer** drives home the point about being **ETDBW** (easy to do business with) in *'The Agenda'*. Add it to your sales library! How easy are you to do business with?

- We continually evolve our primary website **www.ideaman.net** by expanding and enhancing its different customer driven segments. For example, we've added on-line resources and downloadable articles for your reverence.
- *My web work is becoming a series of true value-added client-centric sites, as well as very productive and profitable. It is time well spent in creating time to sell, lead, or manage my business and customer contact relationships.*
- Have you 'systemized' your work area and computers to make it easier for you or your colleagues to access information, client files, literature, etc. to better and more quickly serve your clients?
- Have you spent specific time thinking about all the potential challenges or questions that might come up from a prospective client? Have you discussed these challenges and the productive solutions you and your organization provide? Are your staff fully informed and well 'trained' in helping clients with their challenges? Do you have solid, well-researched, value-enhancing answers ready and burned into your mind? If not, why not?

If you invest even a small amount of time working on these questions and implementing the results of your deliberations – you'll find yourself able to focus more time on the sales, service, and marketing process. You'll also find you will attract more clients, receive better quality referrals, and garner more profitable new and repeat business.

Amazingly enough when you are **'Creating Time to Sell, Lead, or Manage'**, as a part of your customer service focus – you end up selling more and making more money too!

PRO-tips: ABP - Always Be Prospecting!

Never let your sales funnel dry up even when you are crazy busy delivering. One day, that business will end, and you'll be staring at an empty pipeline. Stay in touch, nurture leads. People buy on their timeline not yours.

© **Patti Pokorchak**, MBA, www.SmallBizSalesCoach.ca

Little hinges swing big doors

As I travel the globe, I share a few basic ideas or messages with my audiences. I often tell them, *"Once people fully understand the 'Why?' (purpose) the 'How's?' (processes or procedures) tend to take care of themselves."* Simple little idea, isn't it? However, these little things seem to slip the grasp of many of our North American leaders. We tend to over-complicate things.

W. Clement Stone, who built a billion-dollar *sales* organization out of the depths of the great depression (*early 1900's*) shared a *key* quote that has been close to my own growth and success. He worked with **Napoleon Hill**, who authored, *Think and Grow Rich*, published *Success Magazine*, and mentored **Og Mandino**, who authored motivational classic, *The Greatest Salesman in the World*.

Stone wrote: ***"Little hinges swing big doors."***

Entrepreneurial sales leaders constantly search and are open to finding the next '*slight edge*,' the next profitable idea, or '*little hinge*'. I do too!

What little hinges have you applied in your life to open big doors or opportunities? What hinges have you used to leverage your skills and expertise to better your career, company or community? We trust we have provided a few leverage points for you. What is next for you?

PRO-tips: Never lead with your business card when making a face-to-face cold call. Reach out, shake hands with the receptionist, introduce yourself and ask for his or her name. Comment on something unique in the office and then say, *"I need your help."* When they answer, state why you are there. The objective is **not** to look like every other salesperson that comes in the office.

© **Joe Bonura**, www.bonura.com

Building a successful sales career or profitable business

To be effective in sales and business in general, we must deal with these three critical areas as they directly relate to our clients and their ever-changing needs:

- **Pain**
- **Gain**
- **Sustain**

Your profitability and long-term viability will be impacted to the degree that you work with your clients to affect these diverse areas or concerns. Each area has its focus and resulting profit center.

If we help people with their pain - will they need us when it is gone? This is a good starting point for client engagement. Dealing with their pain should be a solid part of your business, but I would hope you would be able to go a bit further with them.

Helping them gain offers a bit more opportunity to serve and build longer-term mutually beneficial relationships. Clients love us when we help them make gains in their business. **But there is still more!**

If you can work with them through their pain, help them gain in the process, and then take them through by helping them grow and sustain growth, you will be a major part of their team for years.

Repeat buyers are created by building on this three-fold premise. Clients will deal with you time and time again if you help them see and receive the value you provide.

- How do you currently sell in relation to these three areas?
- Are there areas where you know you can make changes in your approach to be more effective in working with your clients for the long haul?

As mentioned earlier, when all is said and done, there are essentially three productive ways to increase your sales or business:

- **Increase the number of clients** you attract and retain to deal with you and your company',
- **Increase the average size of the sale** for each client,
- **Increase the frequency** or number of times each client returns and buys.

Look for ways to attract more clients in the services and product mix you offer. How many reasons can you give them as an incentive or reason to choose you?

Condition your mind to seek creative solutions and/or breakthrough ideas. Investigate other industries. Look at their success stories and best practices and see if they hold a secret that you can creatively transfer to your business.

Fed-Ex simply adapted the central distribution system used by the banking system for his courier delivery. Fed-Ex founder, **Fred Smith**, did well with this transplanted breakthrough!

Often the secret to your success and in your differentiation from your competitors lies in the operations and activities of businesses in a different industry. What can you learn and transfer to yours? Hmmm

As fellow author **Jay Abraham** says: *"Breakthroughs let you outthink, out leverage, out market, out sell, out impact, out defend, out maneuver, and continuously outwit your competition at every level."*

Look for breakthrough or transferable ideas in marketing, innovation, operations, sourcing, technology, systems, process, selling, financing, product mix, service list, and distribution. Every area of your business exists to support what you are doing for your clients. Look for methods or tweaks to make each area serve you and your client.

"To build a long-term, successful enterprise, when you don't close a sale, open a relationship." **Patricia Fripp**

How about looking for ways to add on or cross-sell? This is one of the success secrets of the more effective and profitable selling professionals who maximize every client contact.

Adding on helps you move the client to a larger or superior product, package, or service. It is based on having a thorough understanding of the client's intended use and recognizing that the basic product or service may fail to meet the real needs of your client. Remember, you are committed to their best interests. You are doing your client a disservice if you allow them to buy something that will 'not' meet their needs. Not to mention that when doing so, you are building in a possible unsatisfied result, which will impact your repeat sales potential.

Cross-selling introduces your client to additional products or service. Offer them alternatives that perform better and are in their best interest. Phone service providers like Telus, Fido, and Bell do this well with bundling: Voice mail, call waiting, auto call back, 2nd line, autodial, calling cards, caller ID, 3rd line for security, and 4th line for fax, cable and computer information delivery systems. So, do Bell, Shaw and other telecommunication or media providers.

Test market your product mix and services offered. This single secret from exceptional marketers works at every level in business and sales. Check your marketing or sales messages and tweak them to be more effective.

Experiment with your Website(s), advertising, promotional materials, sales and direct mail letters, live sales presentations and in store demos, guarantees, USP's, pricing points, volume purchase options and discounts, or financing. See what works for you!

Nothing is sacred. Keep refining what you've got until you find something that is effective. Then, continue to update your services and/or products to keep them fresh and relevant to the changing marketplace and evolving needs of your clients.

Look for ways to **form strategic alliances** or co-op with those companies or non-competitive sales reps who are already dealing with the people you would like to attract. Selectively network or collaborate with companies or reps who have already earned your prospective clients' trust and respect.

If you offer complimentary, non-competitive services or products that assist others in better serving their clients, you will find a more favorable response. This can create double wins for you, those with whom you joint venture, and your respective clients who are better served.

You'll frequently see **Starbucks** coffee shops in **Chapters** bookstores across Canada, as well as in many **Canada Safeway** stores. This provides a double win for both companies.

You frequently see bank machines and, in some cases, mini-branches in grocery stores for the same reasons. I've seen **Kinko's** set up in larger hotel complexes and convention centers in the US.

Look for opportunities to offer this kind of connection to people who want to deal with your clients and who offer something you either don't offer or are unable to do so profitably now.

Professional example: Years ago, I came up with an idea for groups of speakers to co-operatively promote and market their services on a regional basis. We each contributed to the creation and maintenance of a website and do some print advertising to self-promote during the year.

Please visit **www.AlbertaSpeakers.com** to see what we have done. We are in our 9th year of working together and most of the speakers on the site have been there since we launched. We have also spun off other geographical speaker promotional websites which do not use paid advertising for promotion. www.TorontoSpeakers.com www.CalgarySeakers.com are two additional joint venture examples. Who would you like to have as a strategic alliance?

Point-to-ponder: ☺

Explore and discuss your ideas on how to apply these principles in your sales process and in how you interact with your current and potential clients.

Mistakes made by NEW, lazy, or ineffective sales staff

- Why is it that some senior or seasoned sales staff are often more effective and productive in their sales efforts?
- Why are some sales staff better at building long-term, profitable relationships that result in repeat sales and multiple referrals?

Could it be that they've learned these simple points that help them sell better and to build more profitable client relationships?

As we have previously discussed, companies and selling professionals that take good care of their clients generally retain them for an extended period.

For ineffective sales staff or newer sales personal that lack the proper training, there are some pitfalls here as well.

Lack of preparation. Someone once said that *"Success happens when opportunity meets preparedness."* Your level of preparedness directly impacts your credibility with a client and can make or break the establishment of a trust relationship. This means knowing your product or service as well as your firm's policies and procedures. It also means having a good understanding of what your competition provides in these same areas. Prepare yourself to win and work to make sure you become a trusted advisor in your client dealings.

Why is it we feel we can simply go through our life and our careers winging it or going with the flow? Why is it so few invest the time to prepare themselves to win, to grow, and to succeed?

Not listening. 90% of salespeople never listen or listen ineffectively and are subsequently doomed to frustration and lack of success in their selling activities. Active listening is the key foundation to discovering your client's current and future needs and to determining your ability to meet them. Asking questions and listening carefully through the interview or qualification part of the conversation is where you build solid foundations for later sales success.

I remember being interviewed by a national Canadian magazine on sales and being asked many questions about closing, overcoming objections, and such. I told the interviewer that, "...most of the situations they presented (examples mentioned by the interviewer) could be dealt with by more effective qualifying. Ask questions earlier in the sales conversation and listen to what your clients tell you. Their answers will provide the guidance you need to help them make effective buying decisions."

Failing to ask for the order. This is the most critical part of your sales conversation. Yet, most of the studies I've read show that 70% of all salespeople never ask for the order. A larger percentage never ask for additional orders. Do you?

I remember asking a group of home furnishing salespeople in Wisconsin, *"Would you like to learn how to double or even triple your sales income in the next year?"* Hands went up across the auditorium. I paused for dramatic effect and told them the secret, *"Simply ask for the order at least twice in the sales conversation."* I went on to say, *"Most of you are not asking even once!"* They were visibly shocked. One of their leading saleswomen told me afterwards that I was right on the money.

Poor or no follow up. Follow up and follow through is where 90% of all great sales are made. Conversely, this is where most sales staff miss the opportunity to gain and maintain a client. This is where the real sale begins (post purchase) and the relationship is built for long-term profitability.

I am continually surprised at how few salespeople follow up on leads or even keep in touch with current clients. A simple act of keeping in touch could provide the leverage to a long and mutually beneficial relationship.

Small Thinking. Want bigger sales? You must think bigger. Ask these questions: *"How high is too high? What is my maximum potential? What is the lifetime value of my relationship with this client? What is the potential for referrals from this client?"*

Think big and act accordingly to see your sales results soar. Dream it and then move confidently ahead to create foundations under your dreams.

Failing to establish and/or maintain rapport. This can be a killer if you have any aspirations of maintaining a mutually profitable relationship over a long period with your clients.

Investing time, at the beginning of your sales conversation, is crucial to your success. Building on that rapport by keeping in touch can separate you from the lackluster salespeople in your field. It will also help attract clients who will become active cheerleaders and champions on your behalf.

Failing to commit and establish oneself as an expert in your field. People like to deal with (and talk about) people who know what they are doing. Failing to present yourself as such negatively impacts or restricts your future earnings with clients.

Do your homework so you know your products, services, and your industry. People love to work with people who know what they are doing and who earn their trust by their demonstrated expertise and credibility. A bit of study now can make a major difference in your future earnings and success.

Ask yourself how you fare in each of these above areas:

- Would you give yourself a passing mark?
- Which areas need a little work?
- How will you change what you do to make sure you give your clients the most professional service possible?

Give your sales team a chance to win by reminding them of these success tactics. Remind them to keep focused and keep working toward their goals of helping the client make a decision that is both good for the client and profitable over the long haul for the company.

How can you change and/or help your sales team make the changes necessary to become a professional salesperson/team and provide continued value-added service?

"Our greatest weakness lies in giving up. The most certain way to succeed is always to try just one more time."
Thomas Edison

Eight tips to dramatically increase your sales income

Most of us in the sales profession are driven or at least led by goals. We set some and some are set for us. One of those goals might be finding ways to increase our sales income and, at the same time, reduce the time demands in doing so. Work less and make more! I love that as a sales goal!

Is this a realistic goal? Yes! One of the best methods to increase your income is to set the goal of turning your one-time clients into champions and regular buyers who come back to purchase from you again and again.

Finding ways to get your potential and current clients to buy in larger quantities is a valuable goal as well. Finding new clients and getting qualified leads and referrals from existing clients is also a valid goal.

Here are some simple sales success tips which will, if applied, allow you to hone your sales skills and confidently move ahead to accomplish these goals.

Become an Avid Reader (Sales leaders are often readers)

Here are two ways to learn new things. One is through your own experience; the other, more efficient way is through other people's experiences. Learning things on your own through trial and error is very costly and time consuming. Leveraging off other people's lessons can be priceless.

There are very few things in selling that haven't already been done before. So why waste your valuable time and money reinventing the wheel? Apply what works and adapt to your specific needs.

Invest in good books, CDs, and DVDs from indisputable sales experts and slash your learning curve. (PS: I have a few other ones that might help. ☺ Visit: www.SuccessPublications.ca)

Top sales professionals are often avid readers in search of new ideas, methods, and training materials to equip themselves to better prospect, qualify, and sell in their pursuit to successfully build a long-term profitable client relationship.

Have Fun Selling

There are plenty of ways to make money out there, so why not pick something you love? Since you spend more time working than any other activity in your life, why not enjoy the time you invest in the selling process? I've seen the difference this approach makes in the productivity of professionals who enjoy what they are doing and have fun serving their clients.

Don't think of selling as work. Approach it as you would any of your favorite leisure activities or sports. Once you get good at what you do, that's what happens anyway. It becomes fun!

Attend Sales Training Seminars

Your future selling success is your responsibility. Don't wait for your company to train you. There is no better way to learn a skill than attending a seminar or selling boot-camp facilitated by successful sales experts.

In addition to the incredible information being shared, you also can network with other success-minded salespeople; both in your industry and in others, where you can learn new ideas that might be successfully transferred to yours.

Ask your management about bringing Bob in to work with you and your team. Visit www.ideaman.net for our sales success programs including one based on this book.

Delegate strategically

90% of your time should be spent meeting with prospects and clients: not doing administrative busy work. Follow-up and paperwork are a part of the process. Check out the section on creating more time for the sales process. Invest in some basic reading or audio products on productivity or time management.

Subscribe to Informative Newsletters

Subscribe to successful selling newsletters and e-zines to keep up to date on hot new techniques and ideas for your business. There's nothing better than getting a regular helping of fresh new ideas and perspectives from experts on selling.

Secret Selling Tips

We invite you to subscribe to our paid online Secret Selling Tips Sales success series to gain new ideas; as well as positive reinforcement in your quest to become a more productive and profitable selling professional. It offers a simple, systematic method to help keep you focused, motivated, and on track to winning in the sales game.

Have the Right Attitude about Selling

The right attitude about selling is what will carry you through regardless of what obstacles are thrown your way. Learning to view prospecting as natural and selling as an ongoing event will make you a sales champion.

Building solid relationships that bring repeat business begins with the right attitude. Your attitude is a key that can unlock doors to success beyond your wildest dreams. The secret is you have full control over your attitude and actions.

A few years ago, I had the privilege of speaking and traveling to several 'have-not' countries. Within five months I was in Iran, India, Mexico, and Cuba. I found, with rare exceptions, the attitudes of the people I met were warm and positive. I found them friendly and willing to serve me as I travelled. Very impressive and notably different than what I so often encounter in North America where we have so much.

Don't Make Excuses for Lack of Selling Success

Under-performers love to have a scapegoat to blame for their failures or lack of achievement. When you talk to them, it is always something: the economy, the competition, the product, or the price… anything outside of themselves.

The truth is, if you really want to become or remain a successful salesperson, you must realize your success, or lack of it, is 100% your responsibility.

Institute a **"No Excuses"** rule in your own sales actions and refuse to accept or listen to the excuses of less professional salespeople. Don't allow those in the whiner's zone (or the loser's lounge) to keep you from entering the winner's zone.

Welcome Your Mistakes as Learning Opportunities

Everyone makes mistakes. Few salespeople consciously correct them. Unfortunately, many salespeople keep committing the same errors in the sales process repeatedly simply because they never take the time to sit down and learn from their mistakes. Don't spend your time worrying or feeling victimized by mistakes. Instead, spend 99% of your time THINK-ing about a creative solution. It works.

Bonus tip: Learn from your successes as well. Even fewer salespeople stop celebrating long enough to clarify *what they did* that helped them succeed or land that big deal. Dissect your successes. If you learn what you did that worked, you can duplicate it with other clients in the future.

What lessons can you leverage?

PRO-tips: Think of your sales meetings with customers as a chess game. You need to be thinking at least 2-3 meetings out. You might want to plant the seed about a new item in development or perhaps an inevitable cost increase. Create content for meetings with customers as a series, not one meeting in isolation. You should always be trying to anticipate what would make the difference down the road. The sales cycle is different from every product, so you need to look beyond and figure out how to wow your customer to get the next order. When I was on the buying side, I looked forward to appointments with suppliers who could help me see the future.

© **Peter Chapman**, www.gpsbusiness.ca

How to turn your sales into profitable repeat business

Many organizations are so preoccupied with securing new clients that they often ignore or pay little attention to their current ones. If your established clients slip away, all the money and effort you invested in getting them is wasted.

By investing time in getting repeat business from your existing clients, you stand to **reap the following benefits**:

- You save on expensive advertising geared to attracting first time clients.
- Existing clients still need your product/service and are therefore your target market for repeat or add on sales.
- You can manage effective mail-out or promotional campaigns.
- You can ask them what they want and work to meet and exceed their requirements. Surprise them with your commitment and retain them.
- Clients who are happy with your organization will frequently tell others and generate the power of word-of-mouth.
- You can make your existing clients an offer which can include their extended network, friends, and colleagues.

Since you have spent your advertising money on getting a new client, it makes good sense to work at keeping that client if you can. For your organization to grow, you need to develop a productive relationship with your clients, so they genuinely feel that your business is looking after them. If they bought from you, they are your target market. It would be folly to forget them.

Chances are good that happy clients will buy from you again and again. They simply need to be reminded of the benefits your business must offer them. A personal reminder that 'you' are there and willing to help works, too. That would be logical, wouldn't it?

As mentioned, US based researcher Jack Parr conducted a survey type study to discover how clients felt about a large, well-known American company's goods and services. He surveyed 6000 clients representing a wide cross section of industries and organizations.

His findings would be representative of typical ratings or results for most companies.
- Two percent of clients surveyed said goods and services were, at best, "poor";
- Five percent rated them as "fair";
- Sixty percent rated them as being "good";
- Thirty-three percent rated the company's goods and services as "excellent".

On the surface this seems to represent great client satisfaction and a cause for celebration. After all, 93 percent of the company's clients proclaimed their goods and services were "good" or "excellent". Perhaps?

The next survey question was the definitive one. All 6000 clients were asked: ***"How willing would you be to purchase from the company again?"***

Of those who experienced "poor" goods or services, not one wanted to be repeat clients. This could be expected.
- A mere seven (7) percent of those who rated the company as "fair" would be willing to be repeat clients.
- Sixty-two (62) percent of those who rated them "good" would deal with them again.
- Ninety-five (95) percent of those who rated their goods and services as "excellent" would be willing to be repeat clients.

These results tend to mirror other studies which reinforce the premise of making solid and consistent client service an integral part of the sales process, and not merely an add-on to take care of unhappy clients.

No company will keep all its clients forever. If you take good care of your clients, you will retain them longer. Based on Parr's research, a company with an average client service rating would keep only 68.8 percent of its clients after just one business cycle. In a fierce market, where you face competitors (global) who are committed to improving, an average company must attract 33 percent of its business from new business just to maintain its revenue basis.

Exemplary client service is a solid foundation to business growth and retention of clients and provides a dramatic financial impact on your bottom line. In fact, a study by a Boston based consulting firm, **Bain & Company**, confirmed that the average Fortune 500 Company could "instantly" double its revenue growth rate with a five percent increase in client retention. They went on to conclude a smaller or medium sized company could double its profits in ten years by "simply" increasing its client retention by 5 percent. Interesting parallel, timeline comparison, and results.

> **"Client service is not a 'PART' of your business; it 'IS' your business!" Bob 'Idea Man' Hooey**

What does it cost you to acquire a 'new' client?
$_____ Calculate your overall costs in advertising, processing, sales commissions on new sales, and other expenses for the past year, divided by the number of new clients you or your firm generated that year.

Understanding your client acquisition costs will help you to focus on the value of retaining and sustaining existing clients and the price for ignoring them. Remember, the figure you come up with is generally 5-10 times greater than the cost of keeping a client and expanding the business they do with you.

Keep in mind the life-time value of a typical client for your firm as well. This will help give you a much bigger picture of the impact of acquiring, retaining, and or losing each client.

Point-to-ponder exercise:

To help you measure your potential to secure repeat business, ask yourself the following questions. Discuss your answers with your fellow selling professionals.

- How good is your client service? Where do you think you or your company needs to improve?
- Have you got systems in place to ensure consistency of service and product development? What are they?

- Are you happy with your image – are you relaying the 'right' message? What image do you think your clients have of you? Of your firm?
- What does your organization do for clients that your competitors are not doing?
- Do you make the most of the testimonials from your satisfied clients to keep the momentum going?
- Have your promotional activities in place which target your existing clients and make them feel valued and special? What are they?
- Do you survey your existing clients to help improve your product or service to them? What are they telling you?

So, how did you rate? **What needs to change?** There is still much more to know when it comes to maximizing your potential for repeat business. Keep your existing clients coming back for more and get them to spread the word about your business.

PRO-tips: Convert 'Up-selling' into 'Value-adding'

Here's a subtle tip on 'up-selling' that I learned from my cousin, Dr. Don, a successful Vancouver dentist. When he examines new patients, he goes over any immediate problems. Then he outlines the options available to improve the attractiveness of their smile. **Here's the key** – he then asks the patient, *"Has anyone else ever taken the time to outline these options for you?"* Generally, the patient says, *"No!"* and expresses frustration that previous dentists never bothered. Result: asking, "… if anyone else has taken the time…" helps ensure that your 'up-sell' is perceived to be a value-added service.

© **Jeff Mowatt**, CSP, HoF, www.JeffMowatt.com

Five successful techniques for generating increased sales

Funny thing, as top performing professionals we need to consistently improve on our sales success. **There is no 'static' in selling!** We need to be working on gaining new customers, repeat business, and, of course, referrals just to keep current, let alone move up to the next level. Let's explore five field-proven success techniques you can use to generate an increase in your sales. You'll find them simple to use and effective for building any business.

Adding Something 'New' or improved to 'The Mix'

Every time you add something 'new' to your business, product, or service mix you create another new opportunity to get more sales. Each time you make a tweak or improvement you open a door for new client conversations. For example, something as simple as adding new information on your website creates another selling opportunity when prospects and customers visit your site to access or view the new information. When was the last time you updated your web pages and, at least, changed the dates?

Adding a new product or service to the list of those you already offer can produce a significant increase in sales. Even refreshing in-store displays help create this effect. The added service or product can increase your sales opportunities in three different ways:

- It attracts 'new' customers who were not 'initially' interested in your current products and services.
- It generates repeat sales from 'existing' customers who also want to have your new product or services.
- It enables you to get 'bigger' sales by combining 2 or more items into special package or bundle offers.

Become a Value-added Resource to Your Customers

Look for ways you can be a trusted resource for your prospects and customers. Supply them with relevant, free information on how to do something more effectively, enhance their business, or save money. Refer them to allied professionals who can help them in areas you don't cover or provide.

You get another opportunity to sell something every time they come back to you for help. This enhances your credibility and builds a trust relationship. *For example, with our Secret Selling Tips we added a weekly Motivational Sales Quotes service.*

Separate (differentiate) Yourself from Your Competition

Find or create a reason for customers to do business with you instead of with someone else offering the same or similar products or services. What makes you 'unique'? For example, do you provide faster results, easier procedures, personal attention, or a better guarantee?

Determine the unique sales/service proposition (USP) or competitive advantage you offer to clients/customers that your competitors do not offer. Promote that advantage/benefit in all your advertising. Give your prospects valid reasons to do business with you instead of with your competition and you'll automatically get more sales.

Focus and Promote the 'End-result' or net benefit

Your customers don't really want your product or service - they want the benefit enjoyed by using it. They don't really care about your background, your services, or even your products. What they 'really' care about is the 'results' they get from using you instead of someone else.

For example, car buyers want convenient transportation with a certain image. Business opportunity seekers want personal and financial freedom for themselves and their family. Sales Managers want successful programs (like *'Secret Selling Tips'*) that will equip and motivate their sales teams to be more profitable in the selling game.

Make sure your web pages, sales letters, sales materials, or media are promoting the end-result or true benefits your customers really want and need.

Anticipate and Prepare for Change

Change is the biggest challenge to your sales or business success. The days are history when a business could constantly grow by simply repeating what it did successfully in the past... or even recently. Aggressive, innovative, global competitors and rapidly changing technology make staying with the status quo impossible if you want to survive and remain profitable.

Think about some larger well-known firms that are in trouble or have gone out of business in recent years. In most cases, their 'failure' was primarily due to ignoring changes in technology, customer needs, competition, and changes in the market or other factors that might have been incorporated into their working environment. If they'd been awake and willing to change, they might still be profitable. Now they are dead or near dead!

Expect change and actively prepare for it. Don't wait until your income declines to act. Develop the habit of looking for early warning signs that something is changing. Then aggressively confront it before you start to lose customers.

Hint: Insure yourself against the impact of change by increasing the number of complementary products and services you offer and by using a variety of different marketing methods. Only a small portion of your total business will be affected if the sales of one product fall off or the response to one marketing method declines. Always be adjusting what you do to be more effective in finding and keeping your customers.

- How many of these five field-proven techniques have you overlooked or ignored?
- How many of these are currently being used in your selling or business strategies?
- When will you act on some new ones?

Problems

> ## *PROBLEMS*
>
> *"Each problem has hidden in it an opportunity so powerful that it literally drawfs the problem. The greatest success stories were created by people who recognized a problem and turned it into an opportunity."*
> **Joseph Sugarman**
>
> *"When you approach a problem, strip yourself of preconceived opinions and prejudice, assemble and learn the facts of the situation, make the decision which seems to you to be the most honest, and stick to it."*
> **Chester Bowles**
>
> *"I am grateful for all my problems. After each one was overcome, I became stronger and more able to meet those that were still to come. I grew in all my difficulties."*
> **J.C. Penny**

Problems are a part of life and even more so of being in business. Problems may be why you exist in business. How you view them and deal with them is a pivot point for your long-term profitability and even survival. Soling problems is what keeps you profitable.

What problems do you and your products or services solve for your clients? How can you make sure they know what you offer to help them make their lives, homes, and businesses better or easier?

An idea-rich KEY to generating repeat sales

Let's deal with this business loyalty myth first: There is no 'real' client loyalty. People go where they get the best deal (meaning the best value for their money). Just because your client has purchased from you once, don't be deluded into THINK-ing that they will automatically buy from you a second or third time.

So how do you keep your clients coming back time and again? To answer this important question, take a moment and think about what would keep a client coming back to a business.

One type of relationship can be called a "symbiotic, long-term relationship" because it extends or integrates into the life of a person or into the operations of a business. Of the **four basic types of symbiotic relationships** (operational, emotional, social, or financial), the operational relationship is the most powerful.

Operational relationships exist when the actual work processes of two businesses overlap or boundaries between them merge or blend. The symbiotic relationship has severe perceived and real penalties for breaking off the relationship and, therefore, encourages the client to come back repeatedly, whether they like it or not.

This is the ultimate client relationship and a key to profitably generating repeat sales. If you service them well this has a double benefit in building intertwined, positive relationships. Investigate most highly successful companies and you'll frequently discover that they have developed symbiotic relationships with their clients.

Here are two great examples of companies that have created profitable symbiotic relationships:

FedEx installs computer terminals and/or downloadable software in many of their client's businesses which help to determine shipping requirements, track shipments, and even integrates into the client's inventory, accounting, and order management system to automate the returns process. This essentially forces the client to use FedEx for their express mailing needs.

Their relationship is supported by their performance and commitment to 100% satisfaction. When you think that they process 2.5 million plus packages each day, this commitment is staggering. But if you had 20 people dealing with a package and each did so with only 98% efficiency, the result would only be a 67% accuracy rate. No wonder they have invested so heavily in IT and a hard commitment to this level of accuracy and client satisfaction.

Campbell's Soup has developed a successful vendor-managed inventory (VMI) program with its clients. A VMI program provides continuous replenishment for its clients by monitoring the client's inventory levels (physically or via electronic messaging) and makes periodic re-supply decisions regarding order quantities, shipping, and timing. In effect, Campbell's Soup has literally taken over the entire replenishment function for its clients, and their clients love them.

If you are in the grocery business and your profit margins are low (they are), you are dependent on volume to create profit. Any way that you can cut back on the investment of time (cost) dramatically increases that margin. In providing their VMI service, Campbell's Soup is creating a mutually beneficial long-term relationship.

Conclusion

Take some time to brainstorm how you can create symbiotic, long-term relationships in your business. Think about how you can extend your products or services into your client's life and business so that their cost to change to another provider would be overwhelming. Remember, the most powerful relationship is one in which you and your client's business processes are successfully intertwined.

Point-to-ponder exercise:

Ask yourself questions pertaining to each of the four areas of symbiotic relationships. Your answers will help give you ideas about what you can do to create or enhance a symbiotic, long-term relationship with your clients.

Follow-up is essential if you want to succeed in business

If you want to build long-term repeat buyers and referrals, this should be your first focus with your client relationships.

If you want to be successful, you need to build a system to follow-up with all your (clients) customers. Do you realize the average business only hears from 4% of their dissatisfied customers? According to **Lee Resources**, 91% of unhappy customers will not 'willingly' do business with you again. However, resolve their concerns or complaints in their favor and 70% will give you another chance and deal with you again.

This is where surveys and call backs are essential. If you wait for them to let you know of a 'problem', you will lose their business forever. Check to see what people are saying about you on-line (e.g. Twitter, LinkedIn, Facebook, Yelp, Instagram, etc.).

This 'unfiltered' customer feedback on their experience can be invaluable to the smart business professional. If you are aware of a problem, you have the chance to do something about it and prove you really want to serve them. The fun part: when you fix their concern, many of them move into being raving fans and champions for you.

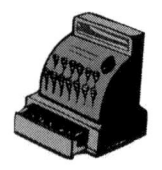

PRO-tips: Conventional wisdom tells us to think outside the box, but there are 7 sides to a sales box and the most important side is often missed in the pursuit of the sale. The 7th Side is the inside! The inside is the human side of sales and connecting with your customer, client or prospect is what builds solid sustainable sales results for long term sales success.

© **Stu Shultz**, www.stushultz.com

What makes 'YOU-nique?'

"To my customer,
I may not have the answer, but I'll find it.
I may not have the time, but I'll make it.
I may not be the biggest,
but I'll be the most committed to your success!"
Anonymous

In a world of increasing 'me-too's' and 'sorta-like's' and 'ditto's' - what makes you stand out from the crowd? What **'YOU-niqueness'** do you bring to the marketplace that will make your potential customers want to deal with you and return time and time again? Are there things you do that your customers aren't expecting? Surprises?

Take a few minutes and give some creative thought to these questions. Analyze your answers, for in them are revealed the secrets of your eventual success and competitive edge.

- What do I provide my clients/customers that **they can't get everywhere else**?
- What can I do to follow-up as a thank you to people – even those who don't buy from me now?
- What can I say or give to my customers that will influence them to remember me and the experience they enjoyed with my firm?
- What 'extra-unexpected-value' can I provide my customers after they buy from me?
- What can I give my clients/customers that will totally amaze them – something they would never expect?
- How can I build long term relationships and communicate with clients/customers and their families that will influence them to remember me for years to come?

Point to ponder exercise

Based on careful thought – what changes will you commit yourself to making which will ensure these 'You-nique' factors become part of your daily operation? When will you start? **Start today!**

Reasons people buy and keep on buying

In his excellent book, *"Rapid Response Advertising"* **Geoff Ayling** provides sales professionals with fifty reasons why people buy. Knowing 'why' people make purchases will allow you to position and continually re-position yourself and your company to help them do so. This knowledge will give you an edge to retaining them as long-term clients and repeat buyers.

One of our facilitators regularly discusses his **top 25 reasons** people buy in his client service program. He contends we increase our ability to serve and sell our clients when we see our products and services through their eyes. He challenges his participants to see how many reasons they can give their prospective clients to buy from them… and keep on buying.

See how many of Geoff's reasons already align or fit with your product and service offerings.

Discuss how you might adapt, amend, adapt, or add on to what you currently offer to make yourself a more attractive resource for meeting your client's needs over a longer period. This is one of the secrets of getting repeat business: give your client a valid reason to do so! Perhaps give them more than one!

How about 50 plus reasons! Geoff says people make purchases for these, among other reasons:

- To make more money
- To become more comfortable
- To attract praise
- To increase enjoyment
- To possess things of beauty
- To avoid criticism
- To make their work easier
- To speed up their work
- To keep up with the Joneses
- To feel opulent
- To look younger

- To become more efficient
- To buy (some just like to shop)
- To avoid effort
- To escape or avoid pain
- To protect their possessions
- To be in style
- To avoid trouble
- To access opportunities
- To express love
- To be entertained
- To be organized
- To feel safe
- To conserve energy
- To be accepted
- To save time
- To become more fit and healthy
- To attract the opposite sex
- To protect their family
- To emulate others
- To protect their reputation
- To feel superior
- To be trendy
- To be excited
- To communicate better
- To preserve the environment
- To satisfy an impulse
- To save money
- To be cleaner
- To be popular
- To gratify curiosity
- To satisfy their appetite
- To be individual
- To escape stress
- To gain convenience
- To be informed
- To give to others

- To feel younger
- To pursue a hobby
- To leave a legacy

Sam Deep and **Lyle Sussman**, who wrote *'Close the Deal'* taught the importance of pain and the ways to learn where it resides. If you know exactly, you've got a great starting point for your creativity.

Now that you've got 50 plus ways to win the hearts and business of your prospects, you'll have an easier job of winning sales, repeat sales, and increased profits.

PRO-tips: What's YOUR U.S.P.?

We thought it might be valuable for you to sit down with your team or staff and think about what your Unique Selling/Service Proposition really is. What advantage do you have or need to provide to separate yourself from your competitors locally and globally?

Seriously consider each of these typical USPs. Some might be applicable; many will simply be an 'ME too' response. It's not unique if everyone does it or can offer it. Be willing to dig deep and prove your points here.

- Selection
- Big or volume discounts
- Advice or assistance
- Top of the line (high end)
- Speedy service
- Service beyond the basics
- Convenience
- Better warranty/guarantee (compared to whom?)

"Turns out the ability to ask insightful, thought-provoking questions was the single biggest differentiator between top performers and average reps." Jill Konrath

Client service redefined... as a sales success tool

These are two questions you need to ask yourself and your clients on a frequent basis.

- *"How can I reinvent myself, or my company to better serve and provide for your changing needs?"*
- *"Is there some service or additional product I should be providing to make your experience easier, more rewarding or user friendly?"*

Remember, if you aren't asking these questions your competitors are.

Here are some tools which will help you keep and expand your market edge; tools to keep your clients happy and coming back for more. **Each of these tools is a valid reason to touch base with existing clients, and a chance to generate additional, repeat business.** Why not invest time to develop an account management system that incorporates one or more of these tools? It may provide insights on how to retrain, retain, or remain a long-term supplier or vendor of choice. Use these where applicable:

Client surveys. Checking in on a regular basis to ask a few questions will work wonders. Consider conducting an exit poll as a spot or on-site form of client survey. If you have made the effort to capture their email addresses, free online tools like Survey Monkey have been made even easier.

Telephone polls. Sometimes a quick phone call to selected clients will be enough to keep you informed and current as to how well you are doing. How about calling a month or so after you've delivered your service or product to see how it is going and how the clients are enjoying the product/service? You can bet there aren't too many businesses doing this.

Service calls. These are a neglected source of information as to the true satisfaction levels of your clients and the serviceability of your products. Enlist your service team as part of your information gathering team and apply what you learn to make your business better.

When I was in the kitchen design business, I used service calls as a way of determining how well we did in serving our clients. I would call each client about a month after we had finished installing their new kitchen and arrange for one of my installers to come for a visit. They were to do routine adjustments on the hardware and cabinets; at least that is what I told the clients. My installers were instructed to find out what the clients liked and to find out if there were any adjustments or areas of concern. I told them, "They'll tell you things they won't want to tell me, because they like me. Find out and fix them on site or if something needs to be replaced let me know and we will order it and you can go back and fix it. I want them to be fully satisfied."

Focus groups. Invest time and invite a few of your best clients to sit down and discuss honestly what you offer and what you deliver. Put your ego on hold and listen carefully as they give you a very valuable gift' a gift that will help you succeed. If you feel nervous about this, hire a professional to facilitate this group program and report back on what they said.

Product sampling. What a great way to find out what your clients want and what you can provide professionally and profitably. This allows you to test market and adjust before you go full tilt into a new product, upgrade, or service roll out.

Website feedback. This is emerging as a great way to allow your clients to tell you how you are doing: what they like, what they don't like, and what they would like. It is a terrific way to share suggestions, changes, and updates with your clients at their convenience. Often clients will share ideas that will solve problems for each other as well.

Invest in your business' future by asking questions and then acting on the responses that your clients provide. This might just be the competitive sales edge you need as we navigate the turbulent and volatile field of business in the 21st Century.

Point-to-ponder exercise

Discuss how you and your sales and service team can incorporate these tools in your current marketing and sales strategy.

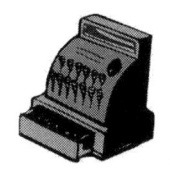

PRO-tips: Idea-rich customer service tips

Don't just love them and leave them. After you've completed the sale, be available for the follow through. Make sure your in-house co-workers are aware of any special needs your client might have. Make sure you are accessible if your client has any questions. Follow up when appropriate to make sure things are going smoothly. Continue making your clients feel like they are the most important clients your firm has; often, based on referrals, they will be.

Customer service can be a value-added sales tool!

Take the extra time to go over the contract, specifications, finance arrangements, and delivery times to make sure you have covered your clients' needs. This is a good time to catch any mistakes, oversights, or *'I thought you said this was included?'* misunderstandings. Change it now and it's an adjustment. Change it later and it's an excuse or a mistake and *unnecessary* stress.

"The fight is won or lost far away from witnesses - behind the lines, in the gym and out there on the road, long before I dance under those lights." Muhammed Ali

Often the battles or challenges you 'successfully' tackle and overcome are dealt with in the privacy of your mind or when you are far from the public eye. This is where character and determination come together for your defense and building the foundation for your emergence as a success, defeating or overcoming your challenges in life. Keep fighting my friends! The long-term business is worth it.

Darren Hardy, publisher of Success Magazine shared a quote from Earl Shoaff that resonated with me, *"The major question to ask on the job is not what am I getting here. The major question is what am I becoming here!"*

Would you buy from yourself?
Conducting an image self-evaluation or audit

"Perception is reality!" This is often the case in business dealings. People prefer to deal with people they like or trust. People base their business perceptions on the image we portray. That image is enhanced or blurred by how we act or present ourselves. This is especially true when looking at the factors that influence people to do business with us on a repeat basis.

☑ Excellent
☐ Very good
☐ Good
☐ Average
☐ Poor

We may be able to sell them once, but how do we ensure that they want to continue dealing with us in the future? **The key question!**

Consider your past six months' experience in dealing with your clients. Take a moment and give yourself some honest feedback on your performance.

Hint: The answers here might show you where you can improve your service and retain clients. Discuss your answers with your fellow sales professionals.

- Is your image one of honesty and straightforward sincerity? How do you know?
- From the buyer's point of view, would you be considered reliable? Why is that true?
- Could you honestly say your clients received special benefits in dealing with you that are not available from one of your competitors? What? Why?
- In your clients' eyes, would you appear to be an expert in your field? Why would they say that?
- Have you been effective in helping solve their problems? How?
- Would you say you handled complaints to their complete satisfaction? How? Share some examples.
- Is integrity one of your values? How does it manifest in your dealings?

- Other than your business dealings, would you think your clients believe you have their best interests and welfare at heart? Why?
- Do clients look at you as a good reliable source of product or service information? Why?
- Would most your clients continue dealing with your business, even if a competitor offered slightly lower prices? Why would they do that?
- What percentage of new clients comes to you from referrals? Why is that number significant?
- How do you plan to keep yourself and your staff educated and current in your field?
- Describe how you keep in touch with past clients. Describe the results.

If you have been honest in your appraisal of your business operation you might have seen a few areas in which there is specific room for improvement.

Go back over your answers and ask yourself:

- How can I improve the way I seek and service my clients?
- How can I change what I offer them to more accurately reflect what they need?
- How can I make a difference in my career and my community by making the changes I see necessary?
- How can I equip my staff and co-workers to better reflect the changes required?
- How can I partner with other business owners to strengthen and expand the way we do business and the services or products we deliver?
- How can I reorganize my business to allow myself to enjoy life better?

Honest reflection, followed by a commitment to act, will perform miracles. Time and time again sales professionals have done some soul searching and come up with some great ways to re-invent their business and give their clients the long-term service they deserve.

> **Because The Customer**
>
> Because the customer has a need,
> we have a job to do.
>
> Because the customer has a choice,
> we must be the better choice.
>
> Because the customer has sensibilities,
> we must be considerate.
>
> Because the customer has an urgency,
> we must be quick.
>
> Because the customer is unique,
> we must be flexible.
>
> Because the customer has high expectations,
> we must be excel.
>
> Because the customer has influence,
> we have the hope of more customers.
>
> Because of the customer,
> we exist.
>
> Author Unknown

The game of sales is best played with enthusiasm and openness. The successful sale professional is one who is always on-the-grow and on the lookout for ways to do it better. Are you?

Pro-tips: *While in the kitchen design business, I tracked my leads. Surprisingly enough, I found we generated 3-5 referrals from happy clients within the first 2 years. That reinforced my attention to detail and making sure each client was fully satisfied with our work.* **How are you doing with your retention and referrals?**

Asking the right questions and finding qualified clients

Questioning, qualifying, or probing skills

Probing is defined in the Webster's' dictionary as the use of a probe (an instrument) to penetrate; usually for the purpose of measuring and investigating. As an action verb, to probe means to interview, to ask questions and to listen, to observe, to study, etc. Probing (qualifying) allows you to accomplish some very important things:

- It enables you to discover what the prospect or client wants and the conditions under which they will buy what you are selling.
- It keeps you from wasting too much time on prospects that will not, or cannot, buy what you are selling under any conditions or now.
- It enables you to discover needs you can profitably meet and suggest ways to meet them to the prospect.
- It enables prospects to identify, clarify, and express their wants and needs.
- It is important to understand the difference between your clients 'wants' and 'needs'. Often, wants are often the impulses that incite their needs.

As professional salespeople we must tap into our client's wants and create an emotional bond that helps make the sale. Re-visit the 50 plus reasons people buy to add to your tool kit. (Page 64)

The secret to qualifying buyers is to find out what they want most. Then give them what they want. You need to discover what they will buy, why they will buy, when they will buy, and under what conditions they will take that action.

Most inexperienced salespeople make the fatal mistake of focusing on what they want from the prospect and not taking time to determine what their prospect wants. Your key to achieving long-term success and generating repeat buyers is in taking a client-centered, value-added approach, enhanced by active listening skills and skillful use of questions to draw out information.

Point-to-ponder exercise

Script out some questions that will effectively mine the information you require for your specific product or service. The answers you receive back should reveal whether you are a correct fit for your client.

When I was starting in the speaking and training business, one of the more seasoned PROs told me to make sure I was the correct fit before discussing the fees. **'FIT before fee!'**

PRO-tips: Only through the awareness of our own distinctiveness can we deliberately and purposefully lead for success. Leadership is about being self-aware enough so that we can be confidently wise, diplomatic, and intentional with competence, embracing the values (and behaviours) of accountability, reliability, and responsibility while being focused. Character and competence are the primary determinants of credibility, with the intention being a part of character.

Credibility is "your reputation" to demonstrate the various characteristics and qualities of being honest, competent, and visionary and the ability to inspire others from our point of view. Credible sales leaders are perceived by buyers as possessing these enduring qualities of trust and expertise. Trust is the foundational component of being credible, which in turn improves our abilities to influence others. Trusted sales professional leaders are more likely to be believed.

Regardless of our level of expertise, if we cannot be trusted by others, we cannot be a credible and effective sales professional.
Before we can build trust and influence with clients or potential clients (or even sales team members), we must understand who we are, what we need to change, and how to go about it. When we are not self-aware about our own preferences, gifts, and talents, it is impossible for us to act trustworthy and influence intentionally.

© **Ken Keis, Ph.D.,** www.crgleader.com

Qualifying 'continued' as a crucial step in your success

Your success in business can 'hinge' on how well you know your competition, your clients/customers, and your capacity to provide solutions that capture their confidence and their business.

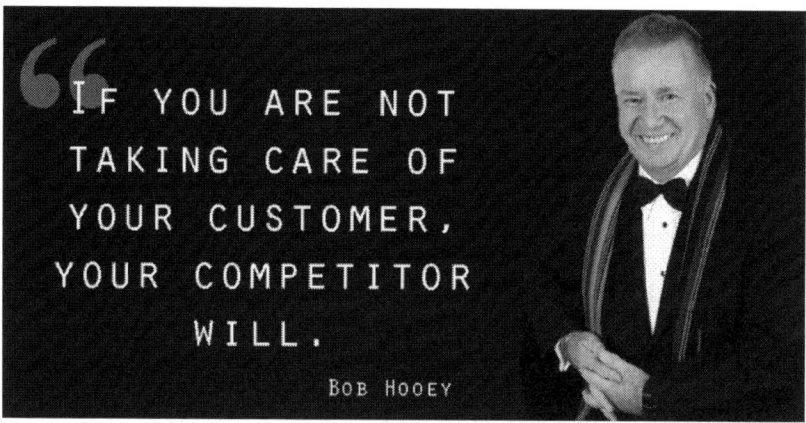

> **IF YOU ARE NOT TAKING CARE OF YOUR CUSTOMER, YOUR COMPETITOR WILL.**
> — BOB HOOEY

This quote has been widely published including an INC. magazine article by Geoffrey James entitled "10 quotes those salespeople should memorize."

As mentioned earlier, sales are lost by rushing through getting to know the client/customer and ignoring their needs and wants in your haste to capture the sale. The secret to becoming successful in selling/customer service is to have a comfortable, systematic and proven qualifying process.

Create and refine your qualifying as a key part of your selling success process and it's easy to increase your revenues and profits without working more hours.

Investing time to dig deeper as part of the client service/selling process achieves two essential things:

- It improves your chance of getting the eventual order or sale by building solid foundations to reveal and help solve your client/customer's problems.
- It sets the stage for a long-term mutually beneficial relationship as well as enhanced customer referrals and repeat business.

"Make your products easier to buy than your competition or you will find your customers buying from them." Mark Cuban

You might want to know:
- **What is the client/customer's problem or opportunity you can solve?** You and the customer are talking about something. He or she is visiting your store or asking you to put a proposal together for some specific reason. What is the problem or opportunity? If there's no problem (challenge, opportunity, supply need, i.e. product or service under consideration), there's likely no sale.
- **What is the financial impact of the customer's problem?** How is the problem impacting them? Is there a way to 'quantify' the dollar amount or value of the problem? It must either be costing him money, wasting his time, or is just inconvenient. Perhaps it is a choice to improve or beautify a living space? How will it fit, how will it look, how will it feel? When you're able to get the customer to tell you how this is impacting their situation, your probability of closing the sale dramatically increases.
- **Who is the decision maker?** Are you talking with the decision maker? If not, it's often a complete and total waste of your time! In retail, who is your customer? When making sales calls, this is even more important.
- **What is the decision-making process?** You need to know how your customer will decide to hire, engage your services, or buy from you. It's always enlightening when you ask, *"What criteria will you use to make your decision?"* Nice to know if they are openly shopping your competition, too. Often, the customer doesn't have a clue or can articulate it. Their answer enables you to ask more questions as you identify and define what is 'really' important to the customer.
- **Where is the sense of urgency?** If there's no sense of urgency nothing's going to happen! Why do they need to buy something? Why do they need to do it now? If you know the answer, you've probably got yourself a sale. If you don't, nothing's going to happen. Is it an advertised sales item or limited time offering?
- **Ask for The Sale!** It's OK to ask for the sale at any stage in the selling /customer service process. In fact, that is your job! Using a soft or trial close is a great qualifying tool to check in with your

customer. Plus, it can be fun to see what happens when you say something like this,
- *"When do you want this item or service delivered?"*
- *"Would you like to sign this agreement [contract, purchase order]?"*
- *"Please sign or initial here."*

Your customer's reaction will tell you a lot about where the sales conversation and your selling/customer service opportunity is really going.

Remember, manage your probe time. Discuss and explore your potential customers' business facts or potential choices: timing, objectives, specifications, etc. quickly. Invest more of your time – 75 to 80% discussing 'their' problems or challenges in reaching 'their' goals, how these problems impact 'them', the cost of doing nothing, the rewards of acting or resolving 'their' issues, and the options 'they've' considered so far. Don't skimp in establishing a relationship or your understanding of their needs, criteria, decision process, or ability to act.

One last hint: Don't be afraid to invest time to educate your potential client/customers on why you provide demonstrably better services, products, or how they work. That too is part of the qualifying process and a great way to demonstrate your expertise and professionalism as well. It builds relationships and repeat business as well.

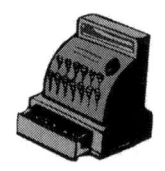

PRO-tips: It's time for you to get brave. Take one of your ideas and TEST IT. Do a pilot project. Do it on a small scale. For a short period of time. Throw it in the sky and see if it flies. Test it on social media and see what the response is. Sell it as an introductory offer and see how many sell. And if it doesn't work, it doesn't sell, it didn't fly? Well – now you know you have some work to do. Some revisions to make. And then you'll test it in a small way again. Don't let the fear of breaking something hold you back. Get that idea out of your head and into reality.

© **Kim Duke**, an international sales expert for women in business. www.salesdivas.com

Finding your ideal client

Knowing who your target market 'really is' can be the secret to building a long-term profitable business. When you know 'who' they are, it helps you understand their needs, what they want, and what goods and services you can profitably provide them. It helps you find them too!

As a business writer, facilitator, and keynote speaker, I am frequently asked about my market, my clientele, and my industry. I am fortunate my creative approach works for professionals across many industries and that I can apply my *'Ideas At Work!'* to help them be more productive in their businesses, associations and careers.

Who is your ideal client or customer? Who would you love to do business with on an ongoing basis? Who would you love to be working with now or in the long term?

Ask yourself:

Who is your ideal client/customer? **Is it...**
- someone who can see the value in what you offer?
- someone who has a demonstrated need for your service or products?
- someone who is open to new ideas and processes in doing business?
- someone who has the ability and the capacity to afford what you offer?
- someone who can buy what you sell?
- someone who will purchase repeatedly from you?

- someone who has a track record or history of working or dealing with someone like yourself or in using similar products or services?
- someone who pays his or her bills on time and is a low maintenance or non-demanding client?
- someone who willingly refers you to other qualified prospects and becomes a champion or center of influence on your behalf?

Sounds like a dream client, doesn't it?

The reality, there are people out there who will match these or other criteria in your search to successfully build your sales career.

Many sales staff neglect spending enough time in the qualifying or interview process. This is where most sales are either won or lost.

- Taking time to ensure your prospect qualifies can make your sales career more than successful; it can transform your platform into a superstar launch pad.
- Take a few minutes to review your best clients and think about what makes them a good fit. Ask yourself what characteristics they exhibit that make them great to work with and why they are frequently your most profitable ones.

If you want to be productive, make a tremendously outrageous income, still have a life, and enjoy the fruits of your labour, this might be a good exercise for you. Invest some time exploring who you would like to have as a long-term client. This works very well.

Point-to-ponder exercise

Discuss the criteria and attributes of your perfect or ideal client with your fellow participants or colleagues. Include areas like personalities and interaction with you in addition to the variety of criteria mentioned earlier.

Getting client feedback using surveys

The most successful companies around the world consistently demonstrate leadership in their client service by asking their clients how they did and what they can do better. Acting on that information to improve or adapt their business process and operating policies is what makes them successful. This allows them to create a competitive edge that keeps them relevant in the minds of their clients and profitable in their activities.

Gaining and retaining your client's trust and keeping them as clients can be a very profitable investment of time and effort on your part. To be effective in this area, it is important to keep the following principles in mind:

Begin with clear objectives. Be very clear about what it is that you want to learn and ask well crafted, targeted questions which will solicit that information. Be specific and give clear instructions on how you would like your clients to respond.

Give your clients a good reason for responding. Rewards work! Offer your clients an incentive for taking their time to give you the valuable feedback you desire: a free offer, a special discount, or a special gift. Make it something they would value – to give you value.

Ask questions that are relevant and important to them. Ask questions from your client's perspective; questions that would be important to their receiving better service, selection, or other areas of importance. This is one time to really put yourself in their shoes, to think and act accordingly.

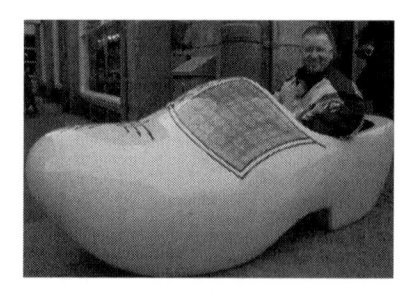

"Bob (in Amsterdam) putting himself in his client's shoes."

Keep it brief. People are busy; more so if they are higher up the leadership ladder. If you make your survey a chore it won't get done. Instead, make it brief, focused, and fun and they will be more inclined to respond.

Confidential self-mailer surveys can generate higher responses. There are times when allowing your clients to answer confidentially will get you what you want. If you are asking questions about your staff, make sure the responses are directed to you and that your clients know they will have your confidence.

If you have collected their emails and have permission to contact them, (be aware of changing spam laws) you might consider using one of the many online survey programs. Many of them are free and can easily be tailored to suit your needs.

Ask easy-to-answer questions. Keeping in mind clients are busy, make your questions quick and easy to answer. A mixture of yes/no, rating 1-10, and open-ended questions will give you the answers you need.

Comments to encourage opinions. Include a few personal comments along with the survey explaining, up front, your reasons for approaching them and your commitment to better serve them. These will work wonders.

Test the survey before sending it out. Just like testing your marketing and advertising, test your survey on a few select clients before you send it out to everyone. Make sure the questions are clear to your clients and that you will get the feedback and answers you really want. Revise it as necessary and then send it.

Focus on your best clients. Remember Parado's principle that 80% of your business is generated by 20% of your clientele. Find out from the clients who shop or stay with you 'why' they do so and what, if anything, they would like to see changed. They've already proven their commitment to your business and are most likely to give you honest feedback that you can use to gain repeat business.

Postcards or an email sent in advance of a survey can arouse their curiosity. One way of improving the response rate of your survey is to let people know that it is coming. Tease them just a little in advance of the actual survey arriving in their mail. This way they will have had a chance to think about their experiences with you and your company and, subconsciously at least, will be better prepared to respond to your request for feedback. Priming the pump will give you better results.

Using surveys as a success tool in finding out more about your client experience can be invaluable.

- Surveys can be one of the most beneficial investments you or your company can make.
- Surveys are a great way to learn how to keep your business fresh and viable.
- They are a great way to discover ways to serve your clients more effectively.

Surveys are also a way to keep you or your company in the top-of-mind category for your clients. They provide the opportunity to keep in touch and remind clients, in a visible way, that you value their input and their continued support and business.

Point-to-ponder exercise

Get together with your fellow selling professionals and brainstorm some specific questions for use to survey your current clients.

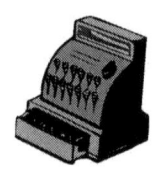

My wife gave me a couple of coffee mugs for our place in the country last Christmas. As I was searching for a point to ponder for our newsletter, I drank from one of them. I paused for a moment to consider its words of wisdom.

"Behind every success is effort...
behind every effort is passion...
behind every passion is someone with the courage to try."
And on the inside lip: "GO For It!"

In the exciting game of sales this is certainly true. Often it is taking that next step to make one more call, one more follow-up or sales letter, that makes the difference. It is taking one more step in the direction of your dreams to capture and create the future you desire. It is taking one more *decisive* step that allows you to pull away from the pack and win and keep the business.

Rules of Value-Added selling and Top-Level service

Being a top-level successful salesperson is a delicate proposition in balancing client needs with maintaining your profitability. Following these rules of value-added selling and top-level service will give you a definitive edge over your completion.

- Client satisfaction is relative to your actual or perceived performance and your client's expectations.
- Client satisfaction is a very subjective thing to measure. It really is a matter of perception and experience. If you meet or exceed the unsaid – unwritten expectations of your clients, their perception will be a positive one. Fail to meet these expectations and you will find them less than satisfied.

One approach to ensure that you meet or beat these unsaid, unwritten expectations is to conduct deeper research. Often, within an industry there are certain *expectations* which serve as the norm. Make sure you know what they are and use them as the bottom line in your service and performance. If you want to succeed in gaining repeat business and client loyalty, make sure you go well past their normal expectations.

There is some business you don't want; but you should value every opportunity to explore the potential of doing business. **When you first start in sales or business, you want to deal with everyone.** This works for the short-term, but not over the long-term. As difficult as it seems, *you need to fire some clients* if the business they bring in is not profitable or is labour intensive to you or your company. Studies have shown that on average, 80% of your business will be generated from 20% of your clients. Yet many sales staff continuously invest their time in those clients who bring the lowest return on their investment.

Trying to be all things to all people is a sure-fire way to go broke. You cannot effectively sell, service, or supply everyone. You need to decide early on 'what business you are really in' and what you can provide profitably to your clients. You cannot service them if you are no longer in business. Sales and its built-in client service is a long-term investment in your business.

Not all clients are valid targets for a value-added effort.

As you develop your sales, decide which clients you can service 'profitably'. Profit is not a bad word; it is the lifeline of your business.

Profit is what differentiates a job or hobby from a sales career.

As you become increasingly clear on what business you are in and what you can profitably provide in the marketplace, you will be better able to target and serve your clients. Selling when you are not able to do so profitably or service in a cost-effective way will detract from the potential you must build into your business. Simply put, if you haven't earned any profits, you have nothing to re-invest to expand your business.

Price is less important when the relationship between the buyer and the seller is strong.

Think about your own shopping or buying experiences: Other than for convenience or disposable goods, where do you shop on a regular basis? Why? Would you drive across town to save a few dollars?

How often would you continue to deal with that company or salesperson even if they are a bit higher in price? Why is that?

When the value of your product and its support and service are evident, and there is a strong relationship built on understanding and trust, people tend to be loyal and will continue dealing with you.

Ask yourself...

- Would you agree that it is often the way you are treated that makes a big difference?
- Would you also agree that often it is the small details than make the difference?
- How can you develop this type of relationship with your clients?
- What would have to change to make it work in your situation?

One final question

How can you apply the lessons learned from your own shopping experience to improve that of your potential and existing clients?

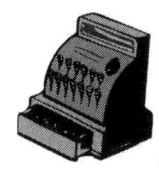

PRO-tips: Growing *Wallet Share*
Are you getting your *share* within existing accounts? probably not. My experience reveals that we often overlook additional opportunities within existing accounts.

Sadly, we succumb to complacency within our loyal accounts and miss out on other revenue sources. Hence, we need to hunt for additional revenue opportunities. I refer to it as growing *"wallet share"*, meaning, how much money do they have in their wallet(s) to spend on your stuff? We often settle for only a portion of their budget, or wallet share. Perhaps the account has separate *wallets* (different decision makers) for additional services you offer but are unaware you exist.

Think of it as nurturing an "account relationship", and not just a "customer relationship". Also, growing *wallet share* would strengthen your position and relationships within that account. That keeps your competitor at bay. Happy hunting.

© **Tim Breithaupt**, www.spectrumtraining.ca

"Think you can, or think you can't – either way, you are right."
Henry Ford

Building foundations for a successful sale

Before anyone buys from you, they typically go through at least four stages:

- You get their attention (the toughest stage of all since we are bombarded with hundreds of marketing messages every day);
- You get your prospect to consider your offer, product, or service;
- Your prospect makes up their mind to buy from you;
- Then, your prospect must act to buy from you.

All four steps take marketing effort on your part. Each step can represent another advertisement or promotional piece you need to buy to march your prospects toward a sale and establish a foundation for repeat sales.

Even after someone buys, they may not come back to buy again. Studies reveal that many people can't accurately remember where they bought things several weeks after the purchase. Current and past clients are the easiest to sell again.

What was the name of the salesman who sold you your last big purchase like a car or a house? Can't remember? You are not alone.

Clearly, you need to stay in touch with the clients you already have. Be sure to include in this group, hot prospects that have shown an interest in your business in the past. These are the most targeted and willing audiences you will ever find.

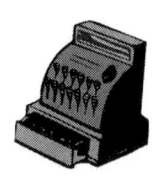

> **Ships at anchor seem peaceful... They were not designed to *just* sit... They were *designed* to sail forth from a safe harbor, to tackle unforgiving seas and uncertain winds in search of other ports... We, too, were *designed* to risk and sail forth...**

When was the last time you took a *calculated* risk? When was the last time you pushed yourself outside of your comfort zone in a sales call? When was the last time you set some seemingly outrageous goals and dared to tell the world about them?

Tell descriptive, idea-rich stories that engage our minds, create value, and help sell on more than one level

Customer service and sales is not 'just' having products or services to sell your clients. It is as much about 'how' you help them experience or investigate potential purchases. It is about being dedicated to helping them make intelligent, value-added decisions that make their life or business better.

Perhaps you've heard or been taught that sharing **Features, Advantages** and **Benefits** is a more effective approach to create 'value' than just feature dumping on our prospective customers or teams. It is! But, do we effectively do that in our sales, service, and leadership conversations?

Let me share a simple experience where a young shoe salesman did this very well.

We all need shoes and hopefully, since we are on our feet a lot, we select some that are comfortable, yet stylish to wear when we are at work. At least that is my story.☺

Years ago, I was doing some sailing in Puerto Vallarta, Mexico. One afternoon I was enjoying a quiet break while window shopping. Along the way, a very stylish, yet simple, pair of two-tone loafers caught my eye in a little shoe store off the quaint cobblestone street. Thinking I was 'only looking'; I stepped into the store to check them out. I picked them up and quickly put them down, as my initial reaction was, *"Wow... they are not cheap!"*

My young and *very wise* shoe expert approached and engaged me in conversation about my visit to his store, to Puerto Vallarta, and what I did for a living. I made the mistake of telling him I was a professional speaker, leadership success coach, and business success trainer who traveled sharing ideas on how others could be more successful in their lives, leadership careers, sales, etc. (Guess he figured I could afford them... smile.)

Picking up the shoes and holding them with reverent care, he said, *"You know, when you wear these traditional loafers, you're going to have a big smile on your face because 'one of the great things' about these shoes is they're soft calfskin leather with a full leather lining. And, as you wear them, they will mold to the shape of your feet, giving you a 'custom-made' feel."*

He continued, *"It would be fun to walk around in custom-made shoes, don't you think?"*

He could have just said, *"These shoes are all leather, which is flexible, making them very comfortable."* On the surface that sounds good, doesn't it?

However, what he said 'engaged' me and was more effective to get me to seriously consider investing in a pair for myself, don't you think? He was **creating value in my mind.** He talked about how the shoes were made. He mentioned they were bench-crafted, which meant one person was completely responsible for making this specific pair of shoes.

Feature (which means)	Advantage (which means)	Benefit (to client)
calfskin leather	molds to your foot	custom made feel
full leather lining	finished feel	instant comfort
traditional loafer	will stay in style	wear for years

He then went in for the sale, *"Since they are bench-crafted, they have the artisan's name on them. When they're finished, these shoes have no nicks, no scratches, and all the components fit perfectly. Unlike shoes made on an assembly line, these shoes are one of a kind."* Now there is a value proposition, if I ever heard one!

Then he asked me a 'simple' closing question, *"What size do you wear?"* He then proceeded to have me slip on a pair in my size.

Long story made short: He was right, they 'are' delightful to wear. When I walked out of his store, both of us had big smiles on our faces. I could hardly wait for the snow to leave back home so I could take them out for a walk here in northern Alberta. I love them! In fact, I took them to Australia that next January for a walk-about.

Simple story of how one young salesman took 'personal leadership' and leveraged his craft to the next level by engaging his client. He told a story that created 'value' in my mind and allowed me to 'see myself' in those shoes.

Do you do that with your customers when they come into your store? Or when you visit them in their place of business?

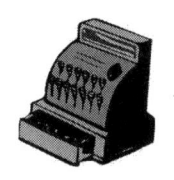

PRO-tips: 1. At the end of each confirmed sale discussion: Thank and congratulate the buyer for their wisdom in taking this action. Then tell them what's going to happen next, paint a positive picture of their "ownership" experience. Ask them to point out how else they can see that this benefits them. Write down what they say, then assure that you make all the "deliverables" come true for them.
2. Ask them, *"What will you tell others about this decision?"* Get their own words to describe dealing with you or obtaining your product or benefitting from your service. Then ask if you can share that with others. Get it on LinkedIn, a letter, a video or an audio testimonial.
3. Create a short document that says something like *"Welcome to the (your company) family!"* Make it something like an owner's manual or new member booklet: tell them of the benefits they'll receive and describe the ownership experience for them. Put all your contact info in there and describe what the "Next Level" of being your customer could be. Show them the "Premium Member" benefits so to speak.

© **Jim Cathcart**, The Motivation Expert www.Cathcart.com

"The key in mastering any kind of sales is switching statements about you and how great you are and what you do, to statements about them, and how great they are and how they will produce more and profit more from ownership of your product or service." Jeffrey Gitomer

How to Up Sell for increased sales and commissions

One of the critical keys to your sales success is up-selling or **'right-selling'** as I like to think of it. It is good to secure the sale; but it is often much better to 'biggie-size' that sale.

Often, this is the 'best deal' for both you **and** the client. Real profits come when you get the client to purchase a larger, more expensive, or a more comprehensive product or service.

As a Sales Professional, are YOU there to help?

Up-selling (right selling) is much easier when you consider your main business as sincerely helping your clients make an informed buying decision. Think about the problems your clients encounter. What does it really take to assist them and to solve their problems? That's your job!

Chances are, your client needs 'substantially' more than the simple inexpensive solution they first consider when approached. By grouping together several different products and services, you can provide the client 'selections and options' to invest in a more advanced package that goes much further toward creating a long-term satisfying solution.

Sometimes you need to suggest a *superior* version of a product that will *better fit* the needs or has the capacity to grow with their needs. It might be more expensive now but cost effective in the long run. They will thank you for being a true professional: selling them what they need and what will best suit those needs over the long haul rather than merely selling them what they ask for.

Three Ways to Make Up-Selling Easy for the Client

Here are some field-proven approaches to build up-selling into any purchase. Use these and clients frequently will buy two or three times as much without even thinking about it. Many professional sales people have seen their sales double and triple by simply incorporating these simple techniques into their normal sales process. What do you have to lose?

Bundle, group, or package several related or complementary products or services together. Drop the price below what the total would be if the client bought all the products separately.

When a client inquires about a single item, investigate what they need and then inform them that they can get that item, plus a great deal more, by purchasing your bundle or special package. You will find many clients can't resist the bundle or package deal bargain.

Announce your new bundle or package deal with flair. You might even come up with a descriptive name for it, like 'the supersaver' system. It can pull in orders faster than you can fill them. Advertising heavily to existing and previous clients who already have a good taste for what you offer is an effective way to boost your sales.

It works fine by itself, but it really works, or it works better when you add this. If your product or service works much better with a complimenting item, be sure to tell clients about it. That is good salesmanship.

It is surprising how many products and services go hand in glove; it's hard to have one without needing the other. If it makes their job easier or meets the client's unspoken needs, you are acting as a true professional in offering them a series of options.

If a little worked, perhaps more or a lot will work even better. As soon as you learn a client is having success with your product or service, offer them a good deal on more (larger volume, bigger supply) of it.

Make sure, of course, that this is in the best interest of your client and will promote a long-term relationship. Volume purchases and agreements can be cost effective but be careful about overloading them; there is potential for that to backfire.

Successful up-selling (right-selling) needs to be at the core of every business or professional practice. It can instantly multiply your profits. You might well go from just getting by, to living comfortably and from living comfortably, to rolling in wealth from happy clients earning you larger commissions, repeat business and lucrative referrals.

Proactive strategies to *minimize* price objections

Wouldn't it be great if price wasn't a factor with your clients? Reality check – it can be or perhaps it might not be the main factor if you work it right. How do you compete when you know you aren't the least expensive in your area? How do you compete in an increasingly competitive global and/or on-line market?

Here are some areas that will help you and your team in this regard.

Strategic Value Analysis: Taking the time to find out a bit about these four areas will help you build a strong foundation and relationship to better service your customers. Better relationships will take the pressure of the price factor in the buying decision. The more you know, the better you can apply that knowledge in serving those who need what you provide.

- **Market Analysis**
- **Competitive Analysis**
- **Self-analysis**
- **Customer Analysis**

Positioning Strategies – to create barriers: Some of the more successful companies have carved out a position as the quality leader in their field. This emphasis on quality or value moves the evaluation process away from price.

Outsmart the competition: Use your brains and look for ways to better 'service' your customers. Find ways to provide services or value-added products that your competition doesn't.

Use all your resources: Being lean and mean in using your resources can help you keep your overhead in line and keep your pricing competitive. Using your resources fully allows you to better serve your clients as well.

Decide on all organizational needs: Taking time to streamline your operation. Keep it simple! This will help your staff provide the best service possible. It also allows your customers to see firsthand your commitment to giving them value for their dollar.

Work to generate end-user support: If you are a supplier – your customers are really your customers' customers. How can you help your customers by working to reach and teach the end users? Become a drawing point for your customers.

Value-added Checklist What do you provide that has value for a potential client? List them now! (List 10 minimum – go for 20)

Bundling: How about making what you offer more valuable by combining products or services to allow your customers lots of options? What types of bundles can you offer?

Proactive probing: Take time to find out what moves your customers. What keeps them up at night? Ask questions and respond to what you learn, by adapting or changing your business. This is one way of keeping what you offer current, valuable, and viable.

Reinforce value: Everything you do should be focused on reinforcing the value in what you offer. What is the true value of what you offer? Warranty, service, selection, delivery, options?

Sell intangibles: Often the true value of what you sell is based on things that can't be shown or proven until needed, as above. Do you have a better warranty? Do you offer better terms? Do you offer a better selection or stocking? Do you offer expert advice or consulting? Do you offer delivery and installation? If so, let them know!

Presentation ideas: When you get an opportunity to present or share about your business or products – I'd suggest looking for ways to incorporate the following areas. You can be a great spokesman if you do.

How can you…?
- Demonstrate earnings
- Cut their costs
- Go for agreement to product first
- Choose your words carefully
- Use proper sales terms instead of jargon

- Sandwich the price – focus on value (good, better, best!)
- Summarize price with benefits
- Cost as a 'mere' fraction
- Minimize the cost-to-own
- Analogize
- Use testimonials wherever possible
- Think and talk long-term
- Present in its best light

"The best way to sell yourself to others is first to sell the others to yourself." **Napoleon Hill**

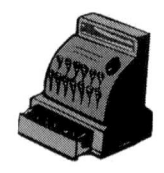

PRO-tips: Knowing Your Competitive Advantages
If you want to be successful in today's market, you need to get the buyer's attention by differentiating yourself, your company and your product. The collaborating phase is where you really differentiate yourself from the rest of your competition. But how do you determine exactly what **your** competitive advantages are? The best way to determine your competitive advantages is to break down your product or service into two distinct categories:

1. **Competitive Advantages:** What can you offer your customers, that the customers value, that no competitor can offer?
2. **Competitive Disadvantages:** Where does the competition have an advantage over you?

How many times have you been in a selling situation where the prospect's sole focus was on price? Anytime your customers **can't tell the difference** between your product or service and your competitor's, they will buy on price. You must differentiate your company, your product, your quality, your service, **and yourself** if you want the prospect to stop focusing on price. You've got to show **how** you are different. So, what are your competitive advantages and disadvantages versus your competitors?

© **Tony Alessandra**, www.Alessandra.com

Checkpoints for Super Sales techniques

Keep these points in mind as you re-enter the field of sales and negotiation with your potential clients. These checkpoints have been pulled from the tactics used by successful top salespeople in various fields. Making sure you focus on being ready to help your clients make informed decisions will make substantial improvements to your bottom line. It will also make a difference in gaining repeat clients and referrals. Learn and earn from the secrets of the professionals in your industry.

We share some of these tips when doing sales training for our clients and their teams. They've found them helpful, hence why they are included here.

YOU and YOUR STAFF play a solid role in laying the groundwork for business success and sales.

- Be neatly groomed
- Smile sincerely
- Keep the work area neat
- Recognize the customer immediately

CARING is demonstrated and appreciated and effective in the business and sales process.

- Be sincere
- Engage a greeting that requires a positive response
- Focus on the customer and the merchandise
- Emphasize a genuine desire to serve

LISTENING is the secret tool used by the superstars – use it!
See the following pages for more information on applying this business building success tool.

- Listen for the message *behind* their words
- Be aware of the customer's body language

TELEPHONE TIPS to build a professional image and support your business connection and sales. Voice connection is an important tool to client attraction and retention.

- Answer promptly and politely
- Put a smile in your voice
- Speak clearly
- Personalize the conversation

MERCHANDISE – being knowledgeable is the secret to being profitable and staying in business.

- Know what merchandise or services your organization offers
- Know where it is located or what is needed to apply it
- Know when and where it is available

BENEFITS/FEATURES – people buy what benefits them!

- Sell the customer the product benefit supplemented with the product features
- Listen to the customer to find out what they consider to be product benefits or features of interest to them

SELLING is both an art and an applied skill that can be honed and enhanced.

- Demonstrate products using a 'you' attitude
- Differentiate between excuses and objections
- Ask only positive questions when closing a sale
- Suggest complementary merchandise that will help the client

KNOW YOUR CUSTOMER to better serve and sell your customer.

- AIDA (attention, interest, desire, action)
- LEAR (listening, empathizing, asking questions, responding)
- Use 'what' questions to draw them out

Build your ABC account management data base

Begin right away to make a list of people who have bought from you in the last week, during the past month, over the past six months, and within the past year. The idea is to develop and maintain different lists so you can send customized or tailored offers to interest and motivate them to buy from you again.

If you clearly see that a big group buys one product or service while another group goes for a different offer, divide your clients up along those lines. With existing account management systems, this is an easy set up.

You can double, triple, and quadruple your response rate by making your ads, offers, emails, postcards, or mail outs zero in on just what a client or prospect is truly interested in buying.

You've heard it before: *"80 percent of your business will come from 20 percent of your clients."* Building your own in-house list and marketing to it consistently will allow you to pull even more business from people who have already proven they like to buy from you.

As discussed, the real benefit here is that you demonstrate your commitment to helping clients on an ongoing basis, while keeping in touch and, of course, inviting them to take advantage of deals, new products, or services. If you are truly a professional salesperson and committed to helping your clients get what they need, you will demonstrate that commitment on a regular basis.

People will respond and reward you with additional orders. They will remember you and refer you to others who can use your products or services.

"You can't build a reputation on what you are going to do."
Henry Ford

Idea-rich secrets to getting great word of mouth referrals and repeat sales

One of the keys to long-term sales success is in developing a client base that will order products from you again and again. The next step is to ensure that the product or service you deliver, not only meets your client's expectations, but far exceeds them. You must 'deliver' demonstrated quality.

Delivering a quality product/service that makes the client glad they dealt with you is not only the right thing to do; it is the real secret to getting favorable product reviews, repeat sales, word of mouth recommendations, and clients who will likely buy your future products/services.

For many businesses, the cost of getting a new client is estimated to be about 5-10 times greater than that of getting an order from a previous client. This assumes that previous clients are satisfied with the purchases they have made from you. If not, you not only lose the 90% savings of having previous clients order from you, you also eliminate the most likely clients for your future products. As well, negative word-of-mouth can sink your sales career or company quicker than anything you can imagine. That's why investing the extra effort to ensure you exceed the expectations of your clients may be the best investment your company can make.

Too many sellers fail to consider the quality of the product/service they deliver to their clients. Instead, they believe it is OK to try to trick the client into buying something shoddy or worthless or something that the client is going to regret buying after they've received it or put it to the test.

It is better to have satisfied clients telling others how great your product/service is than to have dissatisfied clients advising others to avoid doing business with you. Studies have shown that, *"A dissatisfied client can tell 10-16 people about their negative experience."*

Not a pleasant result, and something you can avoid.

Getting your customers to sell you... Creating fans and champions

Over the years, I discovered, *quite by accident,* that my best investment in building my sales and business was in taking very good care of my existing clients/customers. When they are happy and more than satisfied with my products or service, they will talk about me to their friends and colleagues.

Some will even go the extra mile to becoming fans or champions and firmly telling their friends and colleagues that they *'must'* deal with me if they want the best value or service. Wow! Often, they have been instrumental in garnering new business for me as they excitedly share their success or satisfaction with their colleagues and friends.

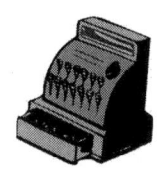

PRO-tips: Secret Selling Tips
Years ago, I had lunch with the CEO of a large Canadian retail firm. I had worked with them for years, training their VPs, helping create a book to reinforce their culture, as well as writing for their internal magazine.

As we came to the finish of our lunch, **Kim Yost** mentioned he needed to find a way to help his 1500 salespeople become more effective, focused, and profitable. We dialogued some ideas and in less than 15 minutes had outlined the basic idea for what would become **Secret Selling Tips.** We launched the English version a month later and the French one shortly after that.

I had approached this challenge to serve this leader, who had become a good friend. What I didn't see was this customer service, business enhancement focus would lead to a completely new on-line business for us. He invited me to share what we'd done with 9 of his counterparts south of the border and 4 of them signed up their entire sales teams too. Wow! This simple sales and service idea started generating an extra $30-50K a year for us.

Go the extra mile – inspired action to separate yourself from your competition

One of the most effective activities in building loyalty and turning customers into repeat buyers, raving fans, and champions of your service or business is to go the extra mile. By this I mean doing more than would be normal to help them achieve the success or satisfaction they wanted.

- Have you ever experienced having someone go way past what would normally be included in your purchase?
- Did it catch your attention and make you take notice?
- How can you do this with your customers?

Do the unexpected – truly amaze them

Companies can build amazing relationships and repeat business. Yet, so few are substantially successful.

- How many times have you been positively surprised in dealing with a salesperson or company?
- They gave you more than you expected or did something you thought would be an extra?
- How did you feel?
- How can you do that in your business?
- Are there some small value-added areas or 'extras' that you can incorporate into your service or product mix?
- How about including some items that other competitors charge extra for or don't offer at all?
- Do you think that would help to create a positive experience in the minds of your clients?

Follow up for complete satisfaction – part of the sales process

One of the areas for growth in providing real value-added service is in the follow-up or follow-through.

How frequently have you had someone you'd dealt with call you a while later to see how you like your purchase and checking to see how it's working?

Sadly, too many salespeople miss a great opportunity to build profitable long-term relationships, by simply following up with prospects or existing clients.

Customer service is PRO-active and deals with the little 'adjustments' before they become major irritants. I think we're scared of the possibility of hearing negative comments or having to go out to fix something. How sad!

The very thing that can turn customers into loyal fans and we're afraid to do it. Many of the most successful companies have a 100% complete satisfaction – whatever it takes policy. Do you? How will you incorporate this area of customer service into your process?

Keep in touch – top of mind means additional sales and business

On a parallel path, how many companies can you think of that have taken the time to keep in touch with you after you've finished paying for the service or product? Sadly, again, very few!

Part of building a positive relationship and turning customers into loyal fans and enthusiastic champions can be simply taking a positive step to keep in contact. How can you build in an easily maintained system to allow you to track your customers? How will you find ways to keep in touch? What commitment will you make to ensure it gets done?

Challenge
Take a moment and think of some other ways that will help you build those relationships that turn your customers into repeat buyers, fans, and champions. Are there any opportunities you've missed to establish this mutually beneficial type of customer relationship? It is never too late to do what is right and to ask for a second chance.

Keep in mind the potential 'life-time value' potential of your customers. *(I assume by now you have calculated this figure.)*

Delivering quality and getting repeat orders

Don't over hype the product/service in the marketing material. Provide an honest description of the product/service, its attributes, strengths, weaknesses, and potential applications. Make it easy for the client to compare and judge the value.

Treat the client with respect. Each time the client encounters you and/or your company they should come away feeling good about the way they were treated. This includes all phone calls, emails, letters, and personal meetings.

Make yourself easy to do business with by simplifying your process and the number of people a client needs to interact with to have their initial or follow up concerns or needs addressed.

Listen to the client's needs. If you are selling a high-end product and a client calls to ask you questions, take the time to find out if your product is really a good 'fit' with the client's needs. Many times, it is better to say 'no' to a client, and explain why, than to have a dissatisfied client wanting a refund.

Being honest up front may cost you a sale but will often win the client's respect (which may well lead to future sales and referrals). If your goal is to create repeat buyers, building on a solid foundation of integrity is the only way to achieve long-term success.

If you are shipping something to a client, please follow these helpful tips:

Package the product well. If you are shipping a physical product, package it well. Something as simple as adding extra padding and using a heavier box can make a difference. Receiving a package that is falling apart will negatively impact the client's first impression of you and your product.

Include instructions. Typically, upon receipt of your product, the client will want to use it right away.

Make this easy for your clients to do by including "quick start" instructions which show how to get the most out of the product, quickly. When applicable, include a training manual, detailed instructions, a video, or DVD.

Include a cover letter. Every box you ship to a client should include a cover letter thanking them for the order and providing information on how to contact you should there be any problems with or questions about the order. The cover letter will serve to immediately reassure any client that they are dealing with a company committed to client satisfaction.

Include a discount coupon or bonus. One way to encourage repeat business is to provide the client with a discount coupon good for the next order. Consider offering a "$20 off on next order coupon" or a series of coupons. This gives the client an immediate incentive to order from you again. Staples did just that this with a promotion that saved larger buyers up to 20% on purchases in the fall (2016).

Include a listing or catalogue of your other products and services. If you have additional items or services for sale, always include a catalogue listing your options and selections with the order. This shows the client that you are well established (enough to have other products or services) and helps build credibility, trust, and potential for future/repeat business.

Include something extra in the package. When one company shipped videos, they always included a free resource directory, free report, free press pass, or some extra item that would be of value to the client. They mentioned this item in the cover letter included with the product and offered it as a "thanks for doing business with us" gift. Not entirely surprising to the company, many clients called to thank them for the gift and to place another order (using the discount coupon provided). What can you include with your next order?

Ship it quickly. Don't make a client wait any longer than necessary after they place an order. Ship the order the quickest way possible and, if you can afford it, include or absorb the shipping.

Deliver a superior product. Make sure the product purchased lives up to and, whenever possible, exceeds the client's expectations.

Creating a superior product starts with finding out what the client needs/wants and then delivering that product in a manner which they will appreciate.

Listen to your client feedback. As you begin shipping or delivering your product, listen to what your clients tell you.

If you get calls…

- because the product was damaged during shipping or delivery, then you need to work on better packaging or your delivery staff.
- wanting to know how to use the product, then you need to include better instructions.
- about the product not being what people expected, then you need to either upgrade the product or revise your marketing copy.

Your main goal is to **make the client 'happy'** so they will choose to do business with you and continue to do so. If you can do that, you will build a base of satisfied clients who will order from you again in the future. To a sales professional, repeat business represents a major step to building a long-term business. (**"Make ME Feel Special"** from www.SuccessPublications.com for more tips.)

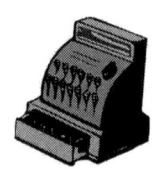

PRO-tips: Video has been one of the most powerful marketing tools I've seen. I've created quick videos and sent them to connections. More than just another email message, video is a rich communication tool to capture words, inflections, facial expressions, and more. People have booked me for business after seeing my videos and asked me to explain how I did it.

Video can also be used to capture a scene or image that you might encounter in traveling. You can send that video with your vocal description to a client informing them of something going on they could use. You become their eyes and ears on the road — a valuable resource for them.

© **Terry L. Brock**, MBA, CSP, CPAE www.TerryBrock.com

The ABC System of effective account management

Let's explore the benefits of developing a workable account management system to manage your accounts. What would your pay-off be for this investment of time and energy? Why would you bother?

Rahul Jacob who interviewed a myriad of Fortune 500 firms and client service experts for Fortune magazine reported the following:

"The real magic of client loyalty is…when you increase it, a beneficial flywheel kicks in. Powered by repeat sales and referrals, revenues and market share grow. Costs fall because you don't have to exert excess energy foraging to replace deflectors. These steady clients are also easier to serve; they understand your modus operandi and make fewer demands on your employee time. Increased client retention drives job satisfaction among your employees, in fact job pride, which leads to higher retention. In turn, the knowledge employees acquire, as they stay longer, increases productivity. The very idea of client satisfaction helps align employees behind a common goal that everyone can understand."

It all comes back to client satisfaction and retention, which leads to a more profitable, long-term relationship of repeat sales. The other benefits cited by Rahul Jacob – employee satisfaction, pride, and retention – simply fuel this on-going client relationship.

But what do we mean by the ABC system?

It could stand for **"Always Be Calling"**. Always making sure you are touching base with your clients to see if there are any additional ways you might be able to serve them. Asking questions about their changing needs allows you to keep abreast of their situation and to anticipate new ways, products, or services you might be able to add to your offerings in maintaining them as a client.

How many of the 50 plus buying reasons (page 64) are you covering? Remember, out of sight – out of mind! Keeping in touch gives you a chance to demonstrate your ongoing client commitment.

The ABC system could stand for **"Always Be Checking in"**. This would imply checking to see how your clients liked your product or service and if there are any adjustments necessary to meet their potentially changing needs.

It could also mean **"Always Be Correcting or Changing"**. In any successful sales career changes in your client base happen. People move on, people get fired, and people get promoted. Make sure your database reflects any changes so you can keep in touch on a regular basis.

Or it could stand for **"Always Be Culling"**. Times change and sometimes it is important to cull or remove, non-profitable or un-reliable clients from your database. Invest your time profitably with clients who can earn you a profit.

Or finally it could simply be to create a simple system you are committed to doing on a consistent basis. As simple as ABC!

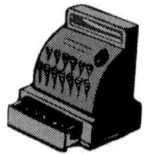

PRO-Tips: Sales secrets to help guide you
- Don't celebrate closing a sale; celebrate opening a relationship if you want to build a long-term successful enterprise.
- It is not your client and prospect's job to remember you. It is your responsibility to make sure they do not have the chance to forget you.
- The real sale comes after the sale, reselling the customer, you must retain their business.

© **Patricia Fripp**, www.Fripp.com

"If you want to reach a goal, you must 'see the reaching' in your own mind before you actually arrive at your goal." **Zig Ziglar**

Getting your clients to sell you

Here are a few idea-rich tips to help engage your clients in recommending and selling you to their friends and contacts.

Go the extra mile
One of the most effective activities in building loyalty and turning clients into repeat buyers, raving fans, and champions of your service or business is to go the extra mile. By this we mean doing more than normal to help them achieve the success or satisfaction they really wanted.

- Have you ever experienced having someone going way beyond what would normally be included in your purchase?
- Did it catch your attention and make you take notice?
- How can you do this with your clients?

Do the unexpected
Remember the last time you were positively surprised in dealing with a salesperson or company. They gave you more than you expected or did something you thought would be an extra. WOW!

- How did you feel?
- How can you do that in your business?
- Are there some small value-added areas or 'extras' that you can incorporate into your service or product mix?
- How about including some items that other competitors either charge extra for, or don't offer at all?
- Do you think that would help to create a positive experience in the minds of your clients?

Follow-up for complete satisfaction
One of the areas for growth in providing real value-added service is in the follow-up or follow-through. How frequently have you had someone call you shortly after a purchase to see how you like it and how it is working for you?

Sadly, too many salespeople miss a great opportunity to build profitable long-term relationships by neglecting to follow-up. Client service is PRO-active and entails dealing with minor adjustments before they become major irritants.

Don't be afraid of opening yourself up to the possibility of hearing negative comments or having to go out to fix something. Consider it an opportunity for growth.

Many of the most successful companies have a "100% complete satisfaction – whatever it takes" policy. Do you? How will you incorporate this area of client service into your process?

Keep in touch
On a parallel path, how many companies can you think of that have taken the time to keep in touch with you after you've finished paying for the service or product? Again, and to their detriment, very few.

Part of building a positive relationship and turning clients into loyal fans and enthusiastic champions simply involves making the effort to keep in contact.

- How can you build in a system which will allow you to track your clients?
- How will you find ways to keep in touch?
- What commitment will you make to ensure it gets done?

Point-to-ponder exercise

Take a moment to consider additional things that you might do to build the kind of client relations that turn clients into repeat buyers, fans, and champions. Are there any opportunities here that you might have missed? It is never too late to do what is right and to ask for a second chance. The potential to build lifetime relationships with your clients is there. Explore it.

"Always do your best. What you plant now, you will harvest later." **Og Mandino**

Unhappy customers cost you money – lots of money!

Deciding to focus on making your customers feel special can pay off in so many profitable ways', just as 'not taking care' of them can have negative results for you and the survival of your business.

Let me ask you a couple of questions as we move further into our time together.
- What is your average sale or transaction worth? (retail) $_____
- What is your average cost to gain each sale? (overhead) $_____

Take a moment and discover how much each (average) client or customer generated for you over the past year. For a quick estimate, divide your gross earnings by the estimated client/customer count last year. Take your advertising and other related marketing costs and divide by customer count.

Let's consider the value of taking care of each of your customers. But first, let's talk about the real cost of having someone 'unhappy' with your services or products.

A variety of research, (e.g. 2011 American Express survey) reveals that: Unhappy customers tell 10-16 other people about poor experiences, (let's use 10 for an average) whereas, Happy customers tell on average 5-9 other people about good experiences (let's use 5 on average)

Each unhappy customer 'costs' your company the purchasing power equal to the minimum purchasing power of 16 customers.

Potential cost of making a customer unhappy is at least 16 lost customers... as follows:

- Original customer not returning: 1
- Customers lost to sharing 'their' horror story: 10
- Customers not gained through positive referrals: <u>5</u>
  Total customer loss =   16 (minimum)
- Now how much is each 'unhappy' customer really worth?
  16 x $_____ = $_____

- And how much will it take to 'attract' and 'replace' 16 customers? 16 x $ _____ x 6 = $ _____

(Hint: Costs run 6-7 times the annual cost for replacement of a lost client)

Add those two numbers to get a real projection of the value of keeping each customer as a happy client.

Now let me ask you another question. How important is it to train your staff to 'effectively' serve each customer and to be 'empowered' to keep them engaged, happy, and satisfied?

(We cover more about this on page 45)

How much is your business worth? Perhaps you see the reason why so many successful stores have liberal return or service satisfaction policies. What changes are needed to make your policies more client friendly?

What changes would you have to make in your training or policies to ensure you satisfy and retain your customer base? What would it be worth to you to see your customers turned into fans and champions – promoting your business around the world? **What is stopping you?**

Happy, engaged clients/repeat customers are the **life-blood** of any successful business. They don't happen by accident! They are a direct result of your training and promotional efforts and the experience they receive when the meet you face to face or electronically.

Make a commitment today to better serve them!

Principles of power negotiating techniques

In the negotiation process — as a critical part of the sale process — it is imperative to understand the basic principles that make the top sales professionals so successful.

We negotiate everyday: with our family and friends, our co-workers to cover for us, with our employers for salaries and perks, and with our clients for sales.

Following a few basic principles will enable you to negotiate fairly which will, in turn, increase the chances of arriving at a win-win resolution. Fine tuning your negotiating skills will secure you a more Profitable and sustainable sales career.

Here are a few points that will assist you in becoming a powerful negotiator, better equipped in the sales process:

If you are a client-oriented sales professional that plans on being here for the long term, you understand that it is better to focus on how both you and the client can win.

Regardless of what you want, in the end, the other person must be satisfied — or at least feel satisfied — with what they got.

Separate the people from the obstacle inhibiting a mutually satisfying conclusion. Focus on solving problems and not on the emotions arising from the problem. Don't make or take it personally.

Knowing the **negotiation style** of the person you are negotiating with is critical to leaving with a positive outcome for both parties.

Focus on interests, not your positions. Positions can be fixed. Each of you may have interests which need to be met. Fixed items can put your negotiations into a corner.

Keep your emotions in check. Never fall in love with something. Doing so puts you at risk of losing some of your chips in the game.

Don't over-react or get angry. It's not about winning. It's about arriving at a mutual win.

Listen to and question the person you are negotiating with. You may discover a better deal than you even thought possible.

These principles, when properly applied, will increase your chances of concluding your negotiations successfully which means that both (all) parties walk away with an agreement deemed satisfactory. If you are committed to gaining repeat business, this must be the focus and the foundation of your sales and follow-up relationship.

These success principles apply in both personal and professional situations requiring negotiation. They can assist you in having more satisfying relationships and a more profitable career path.

Apply them wisely and fairly.

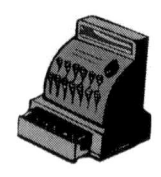

PRO-tips: The two key words for sales success nowadays are 'follow up' and 'value'. The best sales professionals are great at fostering the relationship with their actual clients through their social media presence and their newsletter. 80% of the content they publish, whether it is through articles or videos, is of tremendous value to their clients.

They say: *"I can't believe he is sharing all that great information for free."* Those sales professionals give away tips, ideas, strategies, and solutions that address their client's biggest problems and concerns.

© **Patrick Leroux,** CSP HoF www.PatrickLeroux.com
Entrepreneur, coach, author and Professional speaker

"The difference between great people and everyone else is that great people create their lives actively, while everyone else is created by their lives, passively waiting to see where life takes them next. The difference between the two is living fully and just existing." Michael Gerber

A 60 second reminder

Here are ten quick reminders of ways to be more productive and make better use of your time. Are you serious about exploring ways to create repeat buyers and thereby increase your income through sales? We went deeper with these ideas in **'Running TOO Fast'** (Visit our www.SuccessPublications.ca for more information)

Consistent, wise use of your time will free you up for more face-to-face interaction with current and potential clients and allow more time for the sales conversation and process. This is how you succeed in sales.

Strive for balance and flexibility
Above all, in the process of learning to effectively leverage your time, strive to find and maintain a flexible balance between your personal and business time. This sensible path allows you to be productive, make required changes to regain control of your life, and avoid burn-out for yourself, your colleagues, or your family members.

Strive for personal organization
Maintain focus on the various areas of your life that are important to you. Begin each day by planning and scheduling what is of value for that day. Schedule around your personal energies to ensure the most important and creative activities are scheduled for that time when you are at your best.

Configure your office or workspace for maximum productivity
Your on-site productivity starts with making sure your working environment is ergonomically designed and organized. Reduce the chances of repetitive strain injury (RSI) or long-term loss of energy by ensuring things are within easy reach and located where they offer you the best efficiency.

Learn and leverage using technology
With the advent of improved and cost-effective computers, printers, software, faxes, office networks, cell phones, etc. we finally have access to a whole array of tools which we can use to free up our time. If you are looking for a competitive edge, you will find it by exploring and expanding your use of technology to systemize your business and reduce the repetitive activities to a minimum.

Use your email effectively
Investigate ways of harnessing email to provide ease of access to clients, use autoresponders to answer common questions, and develop more effective ways of maintaining and initiating a true two-way communication with your suppliers, colleagues, and clients.

Use your website wisely
The smarter sales and business leaders are learning how to unleash the power of the Internet and harness the power of their websites by turning them into virtual assistants. Use your website as a client service tool, an information and resource base for potential and current clients. Your website can graphically show your potential clients the depth and scope of your skills, services, and commitment to their success.

Get outside help
As you learn to leverage your time, do what other successful sales and business leaders are doing in increasing numbers – find outside help. Make use of the services of a virtual assistant. Look for ways to outsource repetitive and non-revenue or non-sales generating activities. Perhaps you can work with a colleague and share the load or engage a part-timer who is tasked to free you up for those activities which potentially put you in front of the people who can hire or buy from you.

Leverage your marketing with assistance from others
If you are not marketing, you are marking time, and if so, it is only a matter of time until you are marked for failure. Focus on the most productive form of marketing, your sales efforts. Each client you sell and successfully satisfy can become a self-marketer or champion for you and your services. Ask for help in other areas: such as networking, advertising, direct marketing, and public relations.

Leverage your time by better use of outside services
When you are productively investing your time in the sales and service process, make sure you work to minimize other activities that would distract you or deplete your time or energy. Look for ways to offload personal activities. Consider taking advantage of shopping services, personal assistants, cleaning services, etc.

Use the Internet to its full advantage for services and products you need for your business as well. Many office supply services will deliver to your desk if your order meets certain criteria.

Plan monthly or quarterly, schedule weekly, and live daily!
Set aside time on a regular basis, either monthly or quarterly, to think, reflect, dream, and then focus. Doing so will help you to gain a sense of freedom. Your life, in perspective, will be more productive, flexible, and balanced.

Take the results of that process one step further and use that information to schedule specific time for specific activities on a weekly basis. You will then be able to systematically achieve your goals. You will also be in a great position to live and enjoy your life daily.

Learn and apply some of these time tips and see your face-to-face time increase. If you are spending time on direct sales activities, you will see a marked increase in your sales.

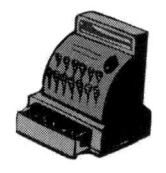

What is your GAP?
If you are like me: Perhaps there is a **GAP** between what you say and what you do? Perhaps there is a **GAP** between what you believe and what is true? Perhaps there is a **GAP** between your dreams and your reality? Perhaps there is a **GAP** between your intentions and your actions?

That is, for the most part, a normal situation in each of our lives. Each of us needs to work on reducing the GAPS in our lives or in filling them if we are truly committed to growing and becoming more productive in our lives and careers.

I'm the nice customer… who never comes back!

"You know me. I'm the nice customer.
I never complain, no matter what kind of service I get.

I've always found people are just disagreeable to me when I do. Life is too short for indulging in these unpleasant little scrimmages.

I never kid, I never nag, and I never criticize. I wouldn't dream of making a scene as I've seen other people do in public places. I think that's awful. I'm a nice customer.

I'll tell you what else I am. I'm the customer who never comes back. That's my *revenge* for being pushed around.

It's true this doesn't relieve my feelings right off, as telling them what I think of them would – but, in the long run, it's a far deadlier revenge.

In fact, a nice customer like myself, multiplied by others of my kind can just about ruin a business! There are a lot of nice people in the world just like me.

When we get pushed far enough, we go down the street to another store. We shop in places where they're smart enough to hire people who appreciate nice customers.

Together we do them out of millions every year.

I laugh when I see them so frantically spending their money on advertising to get me back, when they could have held my business in the first place with a few words and a smile." Anonymous

We don't who wrote this, but it can be a guide for us in making sure we survive and grow our businesses in the 21st Century. It serves as a reminder to treat our clients like the treasures they are and to make sure we give them the value-added service they want and a reason to return and buy from us again and again.

Thanks for reading 'THINK Beyond the First Sale'

Each time I prepare to step on the stage; each time I sit down to write or in this case to re-write, I am challenged to deliver something that will be of use-it-now value to my audiences.

I ask myself, *"If I was reading this, what value would I be looking for?"* As well as *"Why is this relevant to me, today?"*

Thanks for investing in yourself and this Sales Success workbook. These two questions help to keep me focused and clear on my objectives. They help to remind me to dig into my experiences, stories, examples, and research to provide solid information that will be of benefit and help our readers, when they apply it, succeed. That can be an exciting challenge!

I trust we have done that for you in this updated primer to enhance your sales skills. **'THINK Beyond the First Sale'** is my attempt to capture some of the lessons learned first-hand from observing and working with some tremendously effective sales leaders and to share them with you. I'd love to hear from you and read your success stories. If you would be so kind, please drop me a quick email at: bob@ideaman.net

Bob 'Idea Man' Hooey
2011 Spirit of CAPS recipient
www.ideaman.net; www.BobHooey.training
www.HaveMouthWillTravel.com

Connect with me on:
Facebook: www.facebook.com/bob.hooey
LinkedIn: www.linkedin.com/in/canadianideamanbobhooey
YouTube: www.youtube.com/ideamanbob
Smashwords: www.smashwords.com/PROfile/view/Hooey
Follow me on Twitter: @IdeamanHooey
Snail mail: Box 10, Egremont, Alberta T0A0Z0

About the author

Bob 'Idea Man' Hooey is a charismatic, confident leader, corporate trainer, inspiring facilitator, Emcee, prolific author, and award-winning motivational keynote speaker on leadership, creativity, success, business innovation, and enhancing team performance.

Using personal stories drawn from rich experience, he challenges his audiences to engage his **Ideas At Work!** – To act on what they hear, with clear, innovative building-blocks and field-proven success techniques to increase their effectiveness.

Bob challenges them to hone specific 'success skills' critical to their personal and professional advancement. Bob outlines real-life, results-based, innovative ideas personally drawn from 29 plus years of rich leadership experience in retail, construction, small business, entrepreneurship, manufacturing, association, consulting, community service, and commercial management.

Bob's conversational, often humorous, professional, and sometimes-provocative style continues to inspire and challenge his audiences across North America. Bob's motivational, innovative, challenging, and practical Ideas At Work! have been successfully applied by thousands of leaders and professionals across the globe.

Bob is a frequent contributor to North American consumer, corporate, association, trade, and on-line publications on leadership, success, employee motivation and training; as well as creativity and innovative problem solving, priority and time management, and effective customer service. He is the inspirational author of 30 plus publications, including several best-selling, print, e-books, reader style e-pubs, and a Pocket Wisdom series.

Visit: **www.SuccessPublications.ca** for more information.

Retired, award winning kitchen designer, Bob Hooey, CKD-Emeritus was one of only 75 Canadian designers to earn this prestigious certification by the National Kitchen and Bath Association.

In December 2000, Bob was given a special CAPS National Presidential award "…for his energetic contribution to the advancement of CAPS and **his living example of the power of one**" in addition to being elected to the CAPS National Board. He has been recognized by the National Speakers Association and other professional groups for his leadership contributions.

Bob is a co-founder and a past President of the CAPS Vancouver & BC Chapter and served as 2012 President of the CAPS Edmonton Chapter.

He is a member of the NSA-Arizona Chapter and an active leader in the National Speakers Association, a charter member of the Canadian Association of Professional Speakers, as well as the Global Speakers Federation (GSF). He retired (December 2013) as a Trustee from the CAPS Foundation.

In 1998, Toastmasters International recognized Bob "…for his professionalism and outstanding achievements in public speaking". That August in Palm Desert, California Bob became the 48th speaker in the world to be awarded this prestigious professional level honor as an Accredited Speaker. He has been inducted into their Hall of Fame on numerous occasions for his leadership contributions.

Bob has been honoured by the United Nations Association of BC (1993) and received the CANADA 125 award (1992) for his ongoing leadership contributions to the community. In 1998, Bob joined 3 other men to sail a 65-foot gaff rigged schooner from Honolulu, Hawaii to Kobe, Japan, barely surviving a 'baby' typhoon en-route.

In November 2011 Bob was awarded the Spirit of CAPS at their annual convention, becoming the 11th speaker to earn this prestigious CAPS National award. Visit: www.ideaman.net/SoC.htm

Bob loves to travel, and his speaking and writing have allowed him to visit 61 countries so far. Perhaps your organization would like to bring Bob in to share a few ideas with your leaders and teams around the globe. Contact him at: **www.ideaman.net**

Visit:
www.HaveMouthWillTravel.com
for more information.

Bob pictured here presenting at the AFCP conference in Paris, France

PRO-tips: I always say: **"No customers, no transactions!"** In sales, your top priority should be to learn how to make more money through **prospecting**!

If you never confront this aspect of the sales business, you will always be waiting for clients to fall from the sky. Clients acquired like this are so rare that you will work desperately not to lose them when you got them. This vulnerable state of mind is dangerous for a salesperson.

And worse; you can become a victim of your dependence to these few clients who will abuse you and take advantage of your desperation knowing you can't afford to lose their business.

Without confidence and ease of prospecting regularly new clients, you will put yourself in a vulnerable position where you will not be able to reach your full potential for success in sales. And like thousands of others who doesn't want to make this small effort, you'll be one of the sales persons who did a short passage in this job.

© **Sylvia Perreault,** www.slyviaperreault.com

Author's note: *Looking back, I have been selling my whole life. From Cub Scout cookies, Christmas trees, newspapers, to designing kitchens, fabric sales, and lately selling ideas, hope, and help around the globe. Many of these lessons were learned the hard way selling in the trenches. They work if you apply them.*

Copyright and license notes

THINK Beyond the First Sale (updated 3rd edition, 2022)
Idea-rich strategies to attract repeat buyers

Bob 'Idea Man' Hooey, Accredited Speaker, 2011 Spirit of CAPS recipient. Prolific author of 30 plus business, leadership, and career success publications

© Copyright 1996-2022 Bob 'Idea Man' Hooey

All rights reserved worldwide
No part of this publication may be retained, copied, sold, rented or loaned, transmitted, reproduced, broadcast, performed or distributed in any such medium, or by any means, nor stored in any computer or distributed over any network without permission in writing from the publisher and/or author. Care has been taken to trace ownership of copyright material contained in this volume. Graphics are royalty free or under license. The publisher will gladly receive information that will allow him to rectify any reference or credit line in subsequent editions. Segments of this publication were originally published as articles and/or parts of other books and program materials and are included here by permission of the publishers and authors. Unattributed quotations are by Bob 'Idea Man' Hooey.

Cover design: **Wendy** (fiverr.com/craftarc)
Photos of Bob: **Dov Friedman**, www.photographybyDov.com
Photos of Bob: **Frédéric Bélot,** www.fredericbelot.fr/fr
Editorial, layout and design: **Irene Gaudet**, Vitrak Creative Services (a division of Creativity Corner Inc.), www.vitrakcreative.com

ISBN 13: 9781543294293

Printed in the United States 10 9 8 7 6 5 4 3 2 1
Success Publications – a division of Creativity Corner Inc.
Box 10, Egremont, AB T0A 0Z0
www.successpublications.ca
Creative office: 1-780-736-0009

Acknowledgements, credits, and disclaimers

As with each of my books, a very special dedication of this piece of myself, to the two people who meant the most to me, my folks **Ron and Marge Hooey**. Sadly, both my parents left this earthly realm in 1999. I still miss our time together and your encouragement and love. I was blessed with the two of you in my life.

To my inspiring wife and professional proofreader and publications coach, **Irene Gaudet**, who loves, encourages, and supports me in my quest to continue sharing my **Ideas At Work!** across the world. Thank you seems so inadequate for your timely work in helping make my writing and my client service better! I love the time we spend together!

My thanks to the many people who have encouraged me in my growth as a leader, speaker, and engaging trainer in each area of expertise including 'THINK Beyond the First Sale'. People like my friends **Bill Comrie, Kim Yost, and Brian Tracy**.

To my colleagues and friends in the National Speakers Association (NSA), the Canadian Association of Professional Speakers (CAPS), and the Global Speakers Federation (GSF) who continually challenge me to strive for success and increased excellence.

To my great audiences, leaders, students, coaching clients, and readers across the globe who share their experiences and enjoyment of my work. Your positive and supportive feedback encourages me to keep working on additional programs and success publications like this updated version. My experience with you creates the foundation for additional real-life experiences I can take from the stage to the page, the classroom to the boardroom.

My thanks to a select few friends for your ongoing support and 'constructive' abuse. You know who you are. ☺

Disclaimer

We have not attempted to cite all the authorities and sources consulted in the preparation of this book. To do so would require much more space than is available. The list would include departments of various governments, libraries, industrial institutions, periodicals, and many individuals. Inspiration was drawn from many sources, including other books by the author; in this updated creation of **'THINK Beyond the First Sale.'**

This book is written and designed to provide information on more effective use of your time, as a life and leadership enhancement guide. It is sold with the 'explicit' understanding that the publisher and/or the author are not engaged in rendering legal, accounting, or other professional services. If legal or other expert assistance is required, the services of a competent professional in your geographic area should be sought.

It is not the purpose of this book to reprint all the information that is otherwise available. Its primary purpose is to complement, amplify, and supplement other books and reference materials already available. You are encouraged to search out and study all the available material, learn as much as possible, and tailor the information to your individual needs. This will help to enhance your success in being a more effective salesperson, leader or professional.

Every effort has been made to make this book as complete and as accurate as possible within the scope of its focus. However, there may be mistakes, both typographical and in content or attribution. Graphics are royalty free or under license. Care has been taken to trace ownership of copyright material contained in this volume. The publisher will gladly receive information that will allow him to rectify any reference or credit line in subsequent editions. This book should be used only as a general guide and not as the ultimate source of information. Furthermore, this book contains information that is current only up to the date of publication.

The purpose of 'Think beyond the first sale' is to educate and entertain; perhaps to inform and to inspire. It is certainly to challenge its readers to learn and apply its secrets and tips, to challenge them to enhance their skills and leverage their time to create more productive outcomes. The author and publisher shall have neither liability nor responsibility to any person or entity with respect to any loss or damage caused, or alleged to have been caused, directly or indirectly, by the information contained in this book.

Bob's B.E.S.T. publications

Bob is a prolific author who has been capturing and sharing his wisdom and experience in print and electronic formats for the past 20 plus years. In addition to the following publications, several of them best sellers, he has written for consumer, corporate, professional associations, trade, and on-line publications. He has been engaged to write and assist on publications by other best-selling writers and successful companies. His publications are listed to give you an idea of the scope and topics.

Bob's Business Enhancement Success Tools.

Leadership, business, and career development series

- **Running TOO Fast** (8th edition 2022)
- **Legacy of Leadership** (3rd edition 2022)
- **Make ME Feel Special!** (6th edition 2022)
- **Why Didn't I 'THINK' of That?** (6th edition 2022)
- **Speaking for Success!** (9th edition 2022)
- **THINK Beyond the First Sale** (3rd edition 2022)
- **Prepare Yourself to Win!** (3rd edition 2017)
- **The early years… 1998-2009 ATip of the Hat collection** (2020)
- **The saga continues… 2010-2019 A Tip of the Hat collection** (2020)
- **Sales Success Secrets -2 volume set** (2022)

Bob's Mini-book success series

- **The Courage to Lead!** (4th edition 2017)
- **Creative Conflict** (3rd edition 2017)
- **Get to YES!** (3rd edition 2017)
- **THINK Before You Ink!** (3rd edition 2017)

- **Running to Win!** (2nd edition 2017)
- **How to Generate More Sales** (4th edition 2017)
- **Unleash your Business Potential** (3rd edition 2017)
- **Maximize Meetings** (new for 2019)
- **Learn to Listen** (2nd edition 2017)
- **Creativity Counts!** (updated 2016)
- **Create Your Future!** (3rd edition 2017)

Bob's Pocket Wisdom series – *print and epub*

- **Pocket Wisdom for Speakers** (updated 2019)
- **Pocket Wisdom for Leaders – Power of One!** (updated 2019)

Kindle Shorts (2017-2020) series - *more to come in 2023*

- **SPEAK!**
- **LEAD!**
- **SERVE!**
- **CREATE!**
- **CONFLICT!**
- **TIME!**
- **SUCCEED!**
- **WRITE ON!**

Co-authored books created by Bob

- **In The Company of Leaders** (95th anniversary Edition 2019)
- Foundational Success (2nd Edition 2013)
- **PIVOT to Present** (2020) to assist in speaking virtually

PRO-tips: Leaders, Managers, Owners

We'd suggest this book might be a great reference and discussion guide for you and your team. Work through it and discuss where it is relevant in your specific client interaction and culture. Working to create a client centered culture will pay dividends for years to come. We have **'THINK Beyond the First Sale'** available as a lower investment E-pub version as well.

What they say about Bob 'Idea Man' Hooey

As I travel across North America, and more recently around the globe, sharing my Ideas At Work!, I am fortunate to get feedback and comments from my audiences and colleagues. These comments come from people who have been touched, challenged, or simply enjoyed themselves in one of my sessions.

I'd love to come and share some ideas with your organization and teams.

"I've known Bob for several years and follow his activities in business with interest. I originally met Bob when he spoke for a Rotary Leadership Institute and got to know him better when he came to Vladivostok, Russia to speak to our leadership. When you spoke, I thought you were one of us because you talked about our challenges just like yours. You could understand the others, which makes you a great speaker!" **Andrey Konyushok**, Rotary International District 2225 Governor 2012-2013, far eastern Russia

"I still get comments from people about your presentation. Only a few speakers have left an impression that lasts that long. You hit a spot with the tourism people." **Janet Bell**, Yukon Economic Forums

"We greatly appreciate the energy and effort you put into researching and adapting your keynote to make it more meaningful to our member councils. Early feedback from our delegates indicates that this year's convention was one of our most successful events yet, and we thank you for your contribution to this success."
Larry Goodhope, Executive Director Alberta Association of Municipal Districts and Counties

"Thank you, Bob; it is always a pleasure to see a true professional at work. You have made the name 'Speaker' stand out as a truism - someone who encourages people to examine their lives and adjust. The personal stories you shared with your audience made such a great impression on everyone. The comments indicated you hit people right where it is important - in their hearts. Each of those in your audience took away a new feeling of personal success and encouragement." **Sherry Knight**, Dimension Eleven Human Resources and Communications

"Bob is one of those rare individuals who knows how to tackle obstacles in life to reach his dreams. He takes each as a learning experience and stretches for more. His compassion and genuine interest in others make him an exceptional coach."
Cindy Kindret, Training Manager, Silk FM Radio

"Without doubt, I have gained immeasurable self-assurance. Bob, your patience and your encouragement has been much appreciated. I strongly recommend your course to anyone looking for self-improvement and professional development."
Jeannie Mura, Human Resources Chevron Canada

"I am pleased to recommend Bob 'Idea Man' Hooey to any organization looking for a charismatic, confident speaker and seminar leader. I have seen Bob in action on several occasions, and he is ALWAYS on! Bob has the ability to grab his audience's attention and keep it. Quite simply, if Bob is involved - your program or seminar is guaranteed to succeed." **Maurice Laving**, Coordinator Training and Development, London Drugs

"I have found Bob's attention to detail and his ability to fine tune his seminars to match the time frame and needs of the audience to be a valuable asset to our educational Program." **Patsy Schell**, Executive Director Surrey Chamber of Commerce

"Great seeing you in Cancun and congratulations on a job well done. The seminar was a great success! Your humorous and conversational style was a tremendous asset. It is my sincere hope that we can be associated again at future seminars."
Donald MacPherson, Attorney At Law, Phoenix, Arizona

"What a great conference. It was a great pleasure meeting with you at the Ritz Carlton, Cancun and I shall look forward to hopefully welcoming you and your family in Dublin, Ireland someday." **A. Paul Ryan**, Petronva Corporation, Dublin, Ireland

"Congratulations on the Spirit of CAPS Award. You have worked long and hard on behalf of CAPS ...helped many speakers including me and richly deserve this award. Well done my friend." **Peter Legge**, CSP, Hof, CPAE

"I had the pleasure of hearing and watching Bob Hooey deliver a keynote speech several years ago when he gave a presentation at a Toastmasters International Convention. Bob impressed me greatly with his professionalism, energy, and ability to connect with his audience while giving them value. Dr. **Dilip Abayasekara**, DTM, Accredited Speaker, Past Toastmasters International President

Engage Bob for your leaders and their teams

"I have been so excited working with Bob Hooey, as he has given inspiration and motivation to our leadership team members. Both at the Brick Warehouse – Alberta and here at Art Van Furniture – Michigan; with his years of experience in working with business executives and his humorous and delightful packaging of his material, he makes learning with Bob a real joy. But most importantly, **anyone who encounters his material is the better for it."**
Kim Yost, CEO Art Van Furniture, former CEO The Brick

- Motivate your teams, your employees, and your leaders to 'productively' grow and 'profitably' succeed!
- Protect your conference investment - leverage your training dollars.
- Enhance your professional career and sell more products and services.
- Equip and motivate your leaders and their teams to grow and succeed, 'even' in tough times!
- Leverage your time to enhance your skills, equip your teams, and better serve your clients.
- Leverage your leadership and investment of time to leave a significant legacy!
-

Call today to engage best-selling author, award winning, inspirational leadership keynote speaker, leaders' success coach, and employee development trainer, Bob 'Idea Man' Hooey and his innovative, audience based, results-focused, Ideas At Work! for your next company, convention, leadership, staff, training, or association event. You'll be glad you did!

Call 1-780-736-0009 to connect with **Bob 'Idea Man' Hooey** today!

Learn more about Bob at: www.ideaman.net or www.BobHooey.training

Author's note: None of us in sales *deliberately* plans to fail. However, it is quite obvious that *not all of us* in sales are achieving the success we had hoped to attain. Why is that? This has proven to be a global challenge.

I hear all kinds of comments about the 'tough times' we are experiencing and their negative impact on our economies and our lack-luster sales results. I too, see the changes in our economy. However, many of the comments I hear sound more like 'excuses' to me. During these same 'tough times' some salespeople (in industries across the board) are having the best years of their career. **They are making sales not excuses!**

Tough times provide an opportunity to prove your worth and dedication as a selling professional. Your choice!

Tough times give you a chance to shine, to leave your competition in the dust when they run for cover, and to establish yourself as a credible resource and trusted advisor to your current and potential clients. Your choice! **Tough times** can be your most productive and profitable times. Your choice!

I believe one of the reasons we either fail or succeed is *directly* based on our mental conditioning and attitude.
- **Selling** is a lonely, risky, and often challenging business.
- **Selling** puts you in places outside of your comfort zone.
- **Selling** also confronts our fear of rejection on a regular and personal basis.

I believe that top selling professionals are self-created, not born, and that each of us can enhance our selling skills and expertise. Each of us can choose to grow and be more successful in the exciting game of selling when we are willing to invest in acquiring and honing our skills, techniques and keep our attitudes positive. Don't you?

I believe top performers strategically *Think beyond the FIRST Sale* and build long-term profitable relationships.

Bob 'Idea Man' Hooey

> **ONE THING!**
>
> *What 'one thing' have you learned that will help you enhance your sales career?*
>
> *What 'one thing' are you committed to acting on in the next 48 hours?*
>
> <small>Bob 'Idea Man' Hooey — Collector of Wisdom & Creativity Catalyst</small>

My thanks for reading through these pages and at least giving these ideas a thought. My challenge for you is to THINK about which concepts and ideas are appropriate for you and apply them today.

Visit: www.SuccessPublications.ca/BusinessSuccess-Tips.html for special business building success video tips.

"I am not on this earth by chance. I am here for a purpose and that purpose is to grow into a mountain, not to shrink to a grain of sand. Henceforth will I apply all my efforts to become the highest mountain of all and I will strain my potential until it cries for mercy." **Og Mandino**

Made in the USA
Columbia, SC
28 February 2023